ImagiNation

Our Nation shall be born again
And our freedom forever regained.
                                        Debussi Tande

ImagiNation

THEORIZING THE NATION IN POSTCOLONIAL ANGLOPHONE CAMEROON POETRY

Oscar C. Labang

Foreword by
Kashim Ibrahim Tala
Emeritus Professor of Literature

Kansas City, MO

ImagiNation: Theorizing the Nation in
Postcolonial Anglophone Cameroon Poetry
by Oscar C. Labang

First published 2012

Miraclaire Academic Publications (MAP)
8400 East 92nd Terrace, Kansas City, MO 64138, USA

Copyright © 2012 by Miraclaire Academic Publications

All rights for this book reserved.
No part of this book may be reproduced, stored in a retrieval system, or transmitted, in any form or by any means, electronic, mechanical, photocopying, recording or otherwise, without the prior permission of the copyright owner.

ISBN (10): 0-6157-3425-1 / ISBN (13): 978-0-6157-3425-5

Printed in the United States of America

MAP is an imprint of Miraclaire Publishing LLC
www.miraclairepublishing.com

To

Miranda, Gina-Cilia, Kailey and Albright Labang

For their love and care to Daddy

Literary criticism endeavors to form a correct estimate of literary productions. Its endeavour is to see a piece of writing as it is. It brings literary productions into comparison with recognized principles and ideal standards; it investigates them in their matter, form, and spirit and as a result of this process, it determines their merits and their defects. (F.V.N. Painter)

FOREWORD

Anglophone Cameroon poetry, which is the subject of Oscar C. Labang's seminal book, is relatively unknown on the international literary scene. It does not appear in any of the renowned anthologies of modern African poetry. It is not also discussed in any of the major critical works on African poetry. Yet, as the author has argued very convincingly, the poetry does exist and is vibrant. An astonishing amount of good and politically radicalized poetry is being published. More and more debates are also taking place especially among Anglophone Cameroonian writers, scholars and literary critics which centre around the poets' responses to the political moment in contemporary Cameroon. This new approach to the study of Anglophone Cameroon poetry is Oscar Labang's contribution to the on-going debate. More specifically, it is about the intense sense of disillusionment and betrayal engendered by what Cameroonians and their unpatriotic leaders have done with their inheritance.

Theorizing the Nation in Postcolonial Anglophone Cameroon Poetry

The author brings together for the first time seven major anti-establishment Anglophone Cameroon poets who display a vivid sense of history and have a clear conception of their country and the way they want that country to go. All the seven poets are agreed on the fact that there is a crisis of nationhood in Cameroon which originated from the country's chequered political history, and which has been exacerbated by an inept political leadership. The socially engaged poets are particularly irked and flabbergasted by the rapacious use of power, wanton greed, and the absolute lack of responsibility which characterize the political leadership and is destroying the concept of national unity and national integration among Cameroonians. They fulminate against the ruling elite whose official rhetoric revolves around the creation of a unified nation capable of achieving its historic destiny. But, in practice, they worked and are still working towards national deconstruction.

Because all the seven poets are active participants in the drama of social and political change in Cameroon, each poet in his own way has examined the crisis of nationhood and proposed the methods by which Cameroon as a nation can be saved from the brink of perdition. That explains why they use their poetry to raise the consciousness of the people so that they can wake up to the hypocrisy and deceit and work towards the building of a united and viable nation.

That also accounts for why their poetry is essentially realistic and even didactic. Thus, the poets can be said to have engaged in an exercise of deconstruction and construction.

The poets' involvement with political issues naturally raises the question whether politically prescriptive literature compromises aesthetic quality. One literary critic who thinks that aesthetic quality is independent of social determination is Ken Goodwin. According to him,

> For a poet committed to poetry as political instrument, literary quality may seem of little importance: an irrelevance or even a subversive hindrance. It is not surprising, then, that the politicization of African poetry in English has been accompanied by a decline in literary quality.

Oscar C. Labang disagrees with Goodwin's standpoint that the artist's concern should be solely with technical excellence. That is why he decided to judge each of the seven poets by how successful he has been in conveying his message to his audience. We also gather from Labang's analysis of the seven collections of poetry that contrary to Goodwin's contention, the poets under study have succeeded in achieving a unity of form and content. In other words, their polemicism does not affect the artistic quality of their poetry.

Labang's book does not provide a definitive reading of Anglophone Cameroon poetry. Rather, it is written with verve and clarity in order to stimulate the imagination. That is why it is addressed to teachers, researchers and students in higher education who are interested in Anglophone Cameroon poetry.

Kashim Ibrahim Tala
Emeritus Professor of Literature and Ecoculture
University of Buea.

PREFACE

The inspiration to write this book occurred to me in 2009 when I was recruited to teach British Literature and Theoretical Criticism in the Department of English and Literatures of English Expression at the then newly created University of Maroua. During my very short stay in Maroua, I taught a friend's course in the Bilingual Department on Cameroon, Continental and World Literature. In my survey of the critical literature on Anglophone Cameroon writing, it occurred to me that there is conspicuous absence of critical material especially on Anglophone Cameroon poetry. My teaching of Cameroonian poetry, as part of the course, and the realization of the apparent gap in critical enterprise inspired me to sketch out and begin developing two major book projects on Anglophone Cameroon Poetry. The first project was temporarily titled "Voices and Visions" and the second was temporarily titled "Leadership Crises". My travel to the United States provided ample time and resources for the completion of both projects. While the first project is currently being edited, the second developed into this present book.

Though trained as a specialist in Modernist Anglo-American poetry, I have a strong passion for colonial and postcolonial Anglophone Literatures with particular interest in Anglophone Cameroon Literature (poetry) which has been in the wilderness of literary criticism for a good while. After the publication of *Riot in the Mind: A Critical Study of J.N. Nkengasong*, my interest in Anglophone Cameroon literature developed even further. While I take off time to read some Anglophone Caribbean and Australian poetry, much of what I read and write about, besides Modern and Contemporary British poetry, is Anglophone Cameroon Poetry. My personal journal *La Bang* (www.la-bang.org) provides an avenue for me to publish at least one essay (draft) each month on Anglophone Cameroon poetry while providing commentary and review on Anglophone Cameroon Film and Literature in general.

In this book my aim is to explore the various perspectives of nationhood and nationalism, and to illustrate each perspective by analyzing poems from the most typical writers. I have in no way attempted and can in no way claim to have made a complete analysis of what might be thought of as Anglophone Cameroon poetry. What I have done is to analyze poetic works that represent the various perspectives of nation and nationalism with emphasis on the works of some poets from the Second and Third Generations. This study explores the works of seven poets, dedicating a chapter to each poet with the intension of giving each poet sufficient critical attention. Each chapter gives analytical significance to a single poet's vision about an aspect of nationhood and nationalism. It is my ardent hope that the publication of this book will generate and enhance more discussion as well as the spread of critical opinions on Anglophone Cameroon poetry and literature in general.

Conspicuously, but deliberately, this work does not include nationalist sentiments and questions of nationhood from diaspora Anglophone Cameroon poets represented by vibrant poetic voices like Emmanuel Fru Doh, Peter Vakunta, Joyce Ashuntantang, Kangsen Feka Wakai and Dibussi Tande. The first reason for this is that the spectatoral distance and the dual nationality of some of these poets affect their vision of the nation and put to question their identity as poets. Secondly, and more importantly, this group constitutes the subject of a separate ongoing project.

I want to use this opportunity to express my gratitude to Professor Edward O. Ako, Rector of the University of Maroua, for recruiting me to that institution thereby indirectly inspiring the writing of this work. My academic mentor, Professor John

Nkemngong Nkengasong deserves immeasurable thanks for preparing me for the challenges in the world of scholarly thinking. Immense thanks to Emeritus Professor Kashim Ibrahim Tala, Professor Nol Alembong and Professor Shadrach Ambanasom for their ever inspiring comments. I owe sincere gratitude to the Director of Publication at Miraclaire Publishing, Miss Louisa Lum, for making valuable suggestions and commentary. For the permission to use and make copies of their collections, I want to offer my sincerest thanks to all the poets.

Oscar C. Labang (PhD)
Kansas City, MO
October, 2012

Contents

FOREWORD i

PREFACE v

CHAPTER ONE: INTRODUCTION

FROM SOUTHERN CAMEROONIANS TO BEASTS OF NO NATION 1

CHAPTER TWO

THE FOREST: A METAPHOR OF THE NATION IN NOL ALEMBONG'S *FOREST ECHOES* 18

CHAPTER THREE

APOCALYPTIC NATIONALISM: DESTRUCTION AND REBIRTH IN SAMPSON NKWETATANG'S "MALEDICTION UPON THE WICKED" 40

CHAPTER FOUR

LEADERSHIP FAILURE IN POSTCOLONIAL AFRICA: NYAA HANS NDAH'S *MY AFRICA* 63

CHAPTER FIVE

REVOLUTIONARY TENDENCIES IN ALOBWED'EPIE'S *CRYING IN HICCOUGHS* 89

CHAPTER SIX
BETRAYED BOND OF BROTHERHOOD: THE CRISES OF NATIONHOOD IN DZEKASHU MACVIBAN'S *SCIONS OF THE MALCONTENT*...114

CHAPTER SEVEN
"DREAMS FOR TOMORROW": SYMBOLS OF HOPE AND UNITY IN GWEDENG NGALAH'S *THE OLIVE TREE*..........132

CHAPTER EIGHT
EXORCIZING THE NATION: SEARCH FOR DIVINE INTERVENTION IN JOHN NGONGKUM NGONG'S *WALLS OF AGONY* 158

CONCLUSION 175

NOTES 183
BIBLIOGRAPHY 185
Name Index 198

CHAPTER ONE: INTRODUCTION
FROM SOUTHERN CAMEROONIANS TO BEASTS OF NO NATION[i]

> The nature of nationhood and national identity is clearly close to the heart of modern African societies because of the territorial demarcations made by European imperial forces during colonialism in the 1880s and 1890s. (Hungwe and Hungwe, 32)

The poet and the politician are two forces between whom the vision of the nation alternates. The politician is constantly in the struggle to develop new slogans to lure the people into believing that the nation is something beyond their very understanding. The poet is in constant struggle to develop new rhetoric which can free the people from the romantic falsehood of the politician and bring them to new realities about their very existential condition in the nation. Thus, the politician fears that the poet may lay open the foundations of society, and that the curiosity of their quest/search might endanger or ruin the whole fabric of the nation. The statesman, John F. Kennedy understood this well, reason for which he said "If more politicians knew poetry, and more poets knew politics,

I am convinced the world would be a little better place in which to live." (Kennedy). The exploration of issues of nationhood and nationalism in poetry is a worthwhile endeavour.

The nation is a postcolonial (or better still anti-colonial) phenomenon defined in a colonial spirit. That is, it is the legitimate product of the struggle of colonized people towards becoming a postcolonial people. It is what Elleke Boehmer[ii] calls "the most achieved form of self-realisation for oppressed peoples" (185). It is the supposed cohesive and well-formed offspring of the anti-colonial movements. Thus, it is plausible to think that the postcolonial nation in Africa is a stillbirth of the anti-colonial struggles. In the birth of the nation in Africa lay its death – a death that resulted from the imperialists attempt to constitute nations conceived in strictly imperialist definitions and conditioned by the imperialists' consumerist necessity to maintain hegemonic dominion over the nations.

The present Cameroon nation is by the condition of its creation and by its current form a hybrid nation; it is first and foremost a combination of two nations historically known at the time of the union as La Republique du Cameroun and British Southern Cameroons; then by its linguistic configuration it is a coalition of multiple nations struggling to share a common sense of nationness and feeling of national belonging. The measurement of this sense of nationness and feeling of national belonging has been achieved most visibly and profoundly in literature especially Anglophone Cameroon Literature. Anglophone Cameroon poetry seems to apparently be the most nationalist of genres that constitutes much of the interrogation of the nation, seemingly by virtue of the fact that it was, according to Buma Kor, the first genre of writing in which Anglophones engaged (Kor, 62). Within this matrix of the nationalistic character of Anglophone Cameroon poetry, John Nkemngong Nkengasong postulates: "Anglophone Cameroon poetry deals with a peculiar postcolonial political situation in Africa, in which the two peoples of opposing colonial experiences were brought together to form a nation" (1) and then goes on to argue that "during almost 50 years of postcolonial experience, Anglophone Cameroon poetry has articulated a network of historical experiences and visions which explore the irreconcilable union that constitutes the Cameroon nation" (Nkengasong, 1).

Anglophone Cameroon poetry in Bate Besong's words "is the way in which the mythmaker relates to the political and economic conditions of his society as a means of communicating shared experiences" ("Post-Unification Anglophone Exile Poetry"). This poetry therefore constitutes what Timothy Brennan describes as "obsessive nation-centeredness" (Brennan,

64) by which he means that this poetry "formalizes the search for, and maintenance of, the idea and meaning of the nation in postcolonial culture" (Obi Nwakanma, Par. 2).

This current study explores a number of perspectives from which Anglophone Cameroon poets of different generations tackle the question of nation, and argues that the radical and ambivalent stance of some of the poets result from the fact that the imagined nation of British Southern Cameroons has never really come to fruition; they harbour a feeling of nipped decolonization which led to a situation of incomplete nationhood on the part of Southern Cameroons. Thus, Anglophone Cameroon has never really completed its process of decolonization or journey to nationhood. Logically therefore they, Anglophone Cameroonians, are 'beasts of no nation' and their poetry is the poetry of an unknown nation.

When Benedict Anderson[iii] defines a nation as an "imagined political community" (49) he places particular emphasis whether consciously or unconsciously on the role of the imagination in the conception and perception of what the nation is. ImagiNation is the poetics of representing the nation through the imaginings expressed dominantly in poetic forms. It is the "image of the nation" (Anderson, 49) as conceived and perceived by the poet through the power of creativity. Because poets are part of the community and lay claim to more refined facultative powers, they generally perceive the nation in ways that are disparagingly different from others. The imagination here deals with the interplay of the poetic and the philosophic which Nkengasong[iv] distinguishes thus:

> The ordinary of poetic imagination refers to the use of figurative language to create poetry and the creative or philosophic is the subject matter of the poetry. The philosophic imagination employs the poetic images as a device for philosophical speculations about life and this is evident in the imagination's quest for esoteric values in a world beyond real experience. (Nkengasong, 5)

The different poets, equipped with the rare and sublime gift of insight, foresight and hindsight stand on the rungs of the imagination and give varying interpretations of the malaise that has enveloped the postcolonial Cameroonian nation. Through the power of vision, they diagnose the problems plaguing the nation, communicate a shared experience of dominion over the individual and some parts of society and imagine the nation as it ought to be thereby revealing a strong sense of nationalism.

The question of nation and nationalism has been at the centre of much controversy in postcolonial discourse. Leela Gandhi, in *Postcolonialism,* points to Anderson's opinion about the secular agenda in the formation of the nation in Western Europe. Gandhi writes:

> ... Anderson argues that the birth of nationalism in Western Europe is coeval with the dwindling--if not the death--of religious modes of thought. The rationalist secularism of the Enlightenment brings with it the devastation of old systems of belief and sociality embedded in the chimeral mysteries of divine kingship, religious community, sacred languages and cosmological consciousness. (101)

Anderson like others postulates that nationalism essentially makes up for the "existential void left in the wake of paradise". In this sense Gandhi concludes that "The nation, then, is the product of a radically secular and modern imagination" (101). Cameroon as a nation was founded on Western imperialist wisdom and so is an archetypal example of secular imperialist machination. The act of forcing one nation (British Southern Cameroons) to achieve its postcolonial status (remember that I have defined a nation above as a postcolonial phenomenon) by joining another nation (La Republique) that was already experiencing its own postcoloniality, the Western imperialist nations at table in the United Nations were more concerned with the "radically secular" (Gandhi, 101) philosophies of their wisdom than with the "spiritual principle" (Renan) that should guide the founding of a nation. This is perhaps why John Ngongkum Ngong thinks that the nation needs some form of exorcism.

Most Anglophone Cameroon writers think of the Cameroonian nation in terms of a reversal of the Hegelian bias. While Hegel sees the journey of 'mankind' as the story of progression from the darkness of nature into the light of 'History', these poets see the evolution of Cameroon especially Anglophone Cameroon as a progression from light of 'History' into the darkness of nature typified by greed, exploitation and inane banalities. To them, independence and nationhood has brought very little meaning in the existence of the Anglophone because the fruit of this supposed progression into nationhood are domination, exploitation, and decline. One of the major ways through which the poets interrogate the concept of nation through imagination and what it means to the existence of the Anglophone is via recourse to history. Gandhi's statement relating to Hegelian opinion about the nation state and history makes this condition even more evident. Gandhi writes:

> 'History' is the vehicle of rational self-consciousness through which the incomplete human spirit progressively acquires an improved sense of its own totality. In other words, 'History' generates the rational process through which the alienated essence of the individual citizen acquires a cohesive and reparative identity in the common life of the nation. (105)

As mentioned earlier the function of 'History' as defined in this excerpt is reversed. The poets depend largely on 'History' to gain "rational self-consciousness" of who they are in the Cameroon nation. But this sense of history does not lead to "an improved sense of its own totality" (Gandhi, 105). In the context of Cameroon, the politics and poetics of national belonging are typified by absurd superiority beliefs and sentiments of untouchable pride which has given rise to the strong enthusiasm by some citizens to destroy the nation. Most Anglophone Cameroon poets' use of history fails to bring them to the "cohesive and reparative identity". Their persistent return to history in Anglophone Cameroon poetry is typified by feelings of inferiority, insecurity, second-class status, angst and anger. Consequently, they find themselves alienated from the nation in which they are supposed to share a "common life" (105).

The nation to the Anglophone Cameroon writer almost does not exist. What is a nation without a sense of national consciousness? How does an "imagined community" become a nation if the people do not share an equal sense of belonging, and a common sense of identity? Most Anglophone Cameroon writers seem to agree with Bate Besong's evocative and provocative title which suggests that the people have 'progressed' through history from Southern Cameroonians to become 'beasts of no nation'. Anderson states that the nation is imagined as a community because, "regardless of the actual inequality and exploitation that may prevail in each, the nation is always conceived as a deep, horizontal comradeship" (50). Ania Loomba also states in *Colonialism and Post-Colonialism* that "Perhaps the connection between postcolonial writing and the nation can be better comprehended by understanding that the 'nation' itself is a ground of dispute and debate, a site for the competing imaginings of different ideological and political interests" (Loomba, 207). The idea of competing ideological and political interest is a typical characteristic of community life be it a political, social, religious or cultural community. This therefore means that there is bound to be such interests in any community. But what is a nation if these competing interests destroy the sense or feeling of "deep, horizontal comradeship" that Anderson talks about? Although the postcolonial Cameroon nation is beset by strong regional sentiments and segregationist attitudes, considered from Anderson's and Loomba's perspectives it is still a nation. When these problems degenerate to the point where the individual experiences severe problems of belonging, national identity and national integration, then one begins to question the bases of the nation because "It [nation] exists in so far as the people who make up the nation have it in mind or experience it as citizens, soldiers, readers of newspaper (sic), students" (Boehmer, 185). What is the nation to the Anglophone Cameroonians who have been made to understand that they do not share in the same sense of citizenship in the political community; that they are second-class citizens or pariahs that are constantly suspected and must be closely watched?

Ernest Renan provides a definition that gives impetus to the Anglophone Cameroonian's feeling that the Cameroon nation lacks the fundamental values of what makes a nation. Renan defines a nation thus:

> A nation is a soul, a spiritual principle. Two things which in truth are but one, constitute this soul or spiritual principle. One lies in the past, one in the present. One is the possession in common of a rich legacy of memories; the other is present-day consent, the desire to live together, the will to perpetuate the value of the heritage that one has received in undivided form [...] The nation, like the individual, is the culmination of a long past of endeavours, sacrifice, and devotion[v] (43).

Renan's definition provides cardinal directions of what should constitute the "spiritual principle" called a nation – a shared sense of the past and the present, a common "legacy of memories", the yearning to "live together", and the strong resolve to preserve and propagate the national heritage. The past, which according to Renan is the foundation of the nation and rationale of its future, embodies the "endeavours, sacrifice, and devotion" of the people as they continually provide their consent to being one people.

The Anglophone Cameroon writer is overwhelmed by the feeling that these three values necessary for the survival of the nation are the daunting task that Anglophones must perform for the Cameroonian nation to survive. This is typified in a work like Bole Butake's *Family Saga* wherein one character assumes supremacy over the other and makes the other to labour and "perpetuate the values of the heritage" alone. The Kamala and Kamalo relationship is a kind of master/slave relationship and therefore does not provide any basis for them to share a common "legacy of memories" (Renan). Interestingly and little wonder, therefore, that at the end of the play Butake calls for an equal level of "endeavour, sacrifice and devotion" between Kamala and Kamalo because for the Cameroon nation to survive Kamala and Kamalo must share the "horizontal comradeship".

The nationalism of a great number of Anglophone Cameroon poets at some level condones the divisive tendency that is characteristic of some minority people as it is characterized by a stubborn nostalgic fantasy for Southern Cameroons, and an insistent struggle to revive the myth and lore of the people West of the Mungo. However, this is not the expression of Edward Said's idea of over 'nativism' which according to him is detrimental to the sense of nation and advantageous to the imperialist course (*Culture*, 276). These are strong ways of reiterating the binary opposition between the two cultures that make up the Cameroon nation without seeking to turn the two sides against each other. Notwithstanding, the nationalism of the poets is even more forceful in their call for order, equity, justice and fair treatment of all individuals who make up the common life of the nation. The condemnation of the excesses of postcolonial leadership and the call for revolutionary action against forms of leadership that work to destroy the identity of the individual in the nation are also forms of nationalism that are common in Anglophone Cameroon poetry. The hope of the poets is that their poetry will "respond[s] to the urgent task of rehumanisation, of regaining an Edenic wholeness. It becomes a process of reterritorialisation and repossession which replaces the 'twofold citizenship' of colonial culture with a radically unified counter-culture" (Gandhi 112). The writers think that there is an urgent need to do what Desmond Tutu describes in *No Future Without Forgiveness*[vi] as the necessity for the nation to:

> [...] rehabilitate and affirm the dignity and personhood of those who for so long had been silenced, had been turned into anonymous, marginalised ones. Now they would be able to tell their stories, they would remember, and in remembering would be acknowledged to be persons with an inalienable personhood. (Tutu, 30)

If all segments of citizens are not recognized to have the same level of "dignity and personhood" (Tutu, 30), then they cannot share a common "legacy of memories" and so cannot share the "desire to live together" which according to Renan are fundamental to the existence of a nation. It is the desire which fosters the sense of solidarity and sacrifice which Renan considers to be the basis of a nation when he states that "A nation is therefore a large-scale solidarity, constituted by the feeling of the sacrifices that one has made in the past and of those that one is prepared to make in the future" (44). As a nation with two independent pasts and two different cultural heritages, linked only by the general idea of colonial domination, Cameroon needs to reterritorialize, to restore the "spiritual soul" as Renan calls it, and to create what Gandhi calls "a radically unified counter-culture" (112) as a postcolonial people.

This work seeks to show that the poetry of most Anglophone Cameroon poets conveys a dazzling ingenious imagination about the plight and condition of the postcolonial Cameroon nation. This imaginative power belongs to and eventually becomes the sober aspect of truth in the poetic cosmos and literary heritage. The various chapters in this book examine the textual strategies of representing the nation - the ways through which the poets individually create an image of the nation or imagine the nation as they see it and how they seek to restore the loss sense of community. The book analyses the poetry of seven Anglophone Cameroon poets from two generations and does elaborate cross referencing to other contemporaries. From the Second Generation of Anglophone Cameroon poets, the analysis focuses on the poetry of Nol Alembong, John Ngongkum Ngong and Alobwed'Epie and from the Third Generation it focuses on the poetry of Sampson Nkwetatang, Nyaa Hans Ndah, Dzekashu MacViban and Gwedeng Ngalah. While one cannot lay claim to the fact that these poets are the best representatives of their respective eras, one can say with great certainty that they handle the issues in focus with great artistic vigour and commitment. Nol Alembong's *Forest Echoes* provides the rhetorical template for analysing the problems of the nation in terms of the metaphor of the forest and what goes on therein. While Nyaa Hans Ndah's *My Africa* condemns the failure of leaders in postcolonial African nations, Alobwed'Epie's *Crying in Hiccups* makes an open clarion call for revolutionary action against such leaders. The youngest of the poets, Dzekashu MacViban laments the fact that the bond of brotherhood/nationhood that formed the basis of the nation has been betrayed. He regrets that the nation was founded on a "punctured genesis". Sampson Nkwetatang takes the unique approach of apocalyptic literature and through the voice of an old man he pronounces judgment and condemnation on those that have ruined the nation. He ends up with a vision of rebirth through divine intervention. Gwedeng Ngalah and John Ngongkum Ngong take a different dimension in their view of the nation. While equally lamenting the present condition of the nation and decrying the excesses of leadership Ngalah still sees glimmers of hope. Ngongkum Ngong takes upon himself the function of a poet-priest to exorcize the nation of its ills and evils through a search for divine intervention. The syncretistic quality in the selected oeuvres puts them on the platform of analytical focus on questions of the nation.

The analyses of most of the texts in question constitute a textual exegesis of selected poems which express the spirit of the nation or convey the poet's philosophy of the nation or their vision of what the nation should be. The analysis is informed largely by Postcolonial theoretical praxis and interpretive tenets. Postcolonial theory is relevant to the analysis and understanding of nationhood because, like postmodernism, it has deconstructed the grand narratives that conditioned the reading of postcolonial narratives as little narratives understood in the light of master narratives propagated by the colonial powers. Thus, postcolonial theory allows the reader to understand the postcolonial nation in terms of the 'independent' narrative that arises from such nation

(Khor, 16). Within this postcolonial theoretical frame new discourses have pushed for the recognition of minority voices like Anglophone poetry within the nation state. Bill Ashcroft in "Beyond the Nation: Post-Colonial Hope" has argued that in spite of the negative critique of the nation in postcolonial studies, the subject of nationalism and the liberated nation still has centrality. He states that:

> Yet in cultural terms the nation is perhaps an even more ambiguous phenomenon than it has been in the past, and this is particularly so in post-colonial theory. The nation-state has been critiqued in post-colonial analysis largely because the post-independence, postcolonized nation, that wonderful utopian idea, proved to be a focus of exclusion and division rather than unity; perpetuating the class divisions of the colonial state rather than liberating national subjects. However nationalism, and its vision of a liberated nation has still been extremely important to post-colonial studies because the idea of nation has so clearly focused on the utopian ideals of anti-colonialism." (12)

The exclusion and division that has beset the postcolonial nation forms much of the subject of the analysis in this study and so makes postcolonial theory the appropriate theoretical tool. The nation in Cameroon fits what Leela Gandhi describes as an "adversarial confrontation between two competing nationalisms" (*Postcolonial Theory,* 124); in which case one can talk about the dialectical binarism in which the nationalism of La Republique du Cameroun push for claims of hierarchical superiority/supremacy over Anglophone Cameroon nationalism. It is this divisive tendency that has destroyed the assumed post-independence utopia and has orchestrated a critique of nationhood in postcolonial Africa.

CHAPTER TWO
THE FOREST: A METAPHOR OF THE NATION IN NOL ALEMBONG'S *FOREST ECHOES*

Metaphor is a rhetorical trope that achieves its effects principally through association, comparison and/or resemblance. Thus, a metaphor creates possibilities for the understanding of one concept in terms of another concept (Lakoff and Johnson, *Metaphors*). It could also be considered in terms of the understanding of one concept in relation to another. It describes a subject by asserting that it is the same as another otherwise unrelated object. This is what the Cameroonian second-generation poet does in his recently published poetry collection entitled *Forest Echoes*. In *The Philosophy of Rhetoric*, I. A. Richards defines the composition of a metaphor to be made up of two parts: the tenor and the vehicle. To him, the vehicle is the object whose attributes are borrowed and the tenor is the subject to which attributes are ascribed.

The focus in this chapter is to investigate how Nol Alembong employs and explores the image of the forest, drawing close association between the making of the forest and the making of Cameroon, the composition of the forest and the composition of

Cameroon and the experiences of what happens in the forest to what happens in his Cameroonian society. Through association, Alembong projects the different phases that the Cameroon nation has on the international front and on the national front. Also through the forest metaphor the poet traces the historical experiences of his people as well as a representation of the difficulties of living in Cameroon especially as an Anglophone. In Richards' sense of the metaphor therefore "Cameroon" is compared to a forest by describing it with the attributes of "forest"; "Cameroon" is the tenor, and "the forest" is the vehicle. The forest and the Cameroon nation form what Zoltán Kövecses in *Metaphor: A Practical Introduction* calls "two conceptual domains, in which one domain is understood in terms of another". Although Alembong does not make this metaphor as clear as conventional metaphors, a close-reading of his poetry with an eye on history reveals very close levels of association.

The forest is a metaphor for pre-colonial Africa and more specifically pre-colonial Cameroon before the coming of the colonial master. Alembong's forest metaphor in this instance does not conform to imperialistic thinking of the forest as a jungle of evil as portrayed in Conrad's *Heart of Darkness*. Contrary to such portrayal, Alembong's forest shows a sense of inner beauty; of cosmic harmony, and of an original and undisturbed universe set to chaos by the coming of the colonial masters. In the poem "The Beginning" he captures the existential condition of Cameroon before European invasion and shows in very strong imagistic terms that the natural unperturbed universe was disrupted by colonial forces. The poem's three stanza structure is unique and artistically beautiful because they convey in a forceful and convincing manner the three stages in the existence of the forest. The first stanza gives a picture of the beginning and how it was; the second defines the peculiarity of that beginning in terms of a sense of unity and cohesion, and the third introduces the chaos that beset the forest. He writes:

> In the beginning was the forest,
> The forest was with the earth,
> The forest was the earth.

These first three lines of the poem establish an intertextual link between Alembong's allegory of the beginning and that of John in the Gospel of John. The dialogue between both texts is that which seeks to give a definitive meaning to the value that existed "in the beginning". The biblical pattern from the Gospel of John Chapter 1:1 onward is replicated here to give a clear focus to the idea of a beginning in the forest. Alembong draws literary parallels between the Word in John's Gospel and the forest in his Cameroon context. In so doing he aligns the beginning in his

Cameroon cultural context to the beginning in the Jewish cultural context.

In the next five lines, the poet extends the metaphor to capture the reality of pre-colonial Cameroon and other African countries before colonial interruption. The oneness of the forest is symbolic of the unity of Cameroon before German colonization and eventual partition between France and Britain as protectorates of the League of Nations and later as Trust Territories of the United Nations. The following lines reflect the unity:

> The forest was one.
> It had one head.
> It had one mouth.
> It had one eye.
> It had one ear.

There is the transference and attribution of human qualities to the forest. The "head", "mouth", "eye" and "ear" are all human characteristics that are attributed to the forest both as a means of defining the oneness of the forest and as a means of conveying the emotional value of the unity. The personification in these lines is given greater meaning by the anaphora "It had one". The repetition emphasizes the strong bond that existed before the coming of Europeans whose destructive tendency is reflected in the image of the fire. Pre-colonial Cameroon existed as a single entity Rio Dos Cameros during the visit of the Carthaginian and Portuguese explorers and Kamerun under German

colonization. But with the coming of the destructive fire set by the League of Nations and later by the United Nations, the country lost its oneness:
> But the fire came,
> The fire came...

The fire is the divisive force that caused the one Kamerun nation to become what has been referred to variously as La Republique and British Southern Cameroons, East and West Cameroon, and Anglophone and Francophone Cameroon. The last two lines create a distinction between what existed before and the new realities. By expressing the division in only two lines, the poet logically suggests the two parts into which Cameroon was divided by the colonial "fire". The separation of the last two lines from the rest of the poem is marked by the use of the connecting conjunction "But". Here, "But" is used to signal both exception and contrary. As a signal of exception, the "But" shows the coming of the fire to be a unique event that altered the existence of the forest. As a signal of contrary, the full negative effect of the coming of the fire is brought to focus. It is used to connect coordinate elements and to show the contrast that has occurred between the life of the forest as it was in the beginning and when the fire came. The "fire" is the force that disrupts the oneness that existed before in the forest. Again, there is repetition which is intended to emphasize – it highlights the devastating effect of the fire. The choice not to say what the "fire came" and did to the forest is interesting and intriguing because the ills of colonialism are many. Instead of pinpointing a particular ill, the poet chooses to leave the poem open ended thereby inviting the reader to be part of the writing process. The reader has the responsibility of completing the poem as the elliptical ending "..." does not suggest anything in particular. Any reader can therefore attribute any colonial ill to the fire.

In the poem "Forest", Alembong allegorizes the condition of postcolonial nations in the metaphor of what the forest is and what it is not. He employs the dominant technique of appearance versus reality to delve into the complexities of postcolonial African nations. What the outsider sees as the condition of the forest (nation) is contrary to what the insider sees. In the poem he represents different postcolonial conditions:

> A forest is dense
> To those who see it from without;
> When in, we see
> The position of each tree.
>
> A forest is green
> To those who see it from without;
> When in, we see
> The colour of each tree.

> A forest is a chorus
> To those who listen from without;
> When in, we hear
> Each tree singing its own song.
>
> A forest is the home of plants
> To those who see it from without;
> When in, we find
> Nests and the trails of beasts. (2)

Those who see the nation from within and those who see it from without represent two different realities. This brings in the question of position and view in that where one stands determines what one sees. The outsider sees the density of the forest but the insider sees the "position of each tree" (2). Another major phenomenon that the poem evokes is that of individuality versus community. The identity of the community surpasses and drowns the identity of the individual especially from the position of the outsider. Individual identity is more perceivable to those in the inside. The colour of the individual leaf contributes to the overall greenness of the forest as seen by the outsider but it is the one in the forest that knows which leaf is greener than the other. Similarly, like in a musical chorus performance wherein the audience hears good music, the choristers hear themselves and hear each other in their distinct parts. The forest is a chorus, but each individual tree is "singing its own song" (2). To the outsider (foreigner), Cameroon is one united nation, but within the nation each region asserts its distinct cultural identity and experiences its own realities.

The appearance versus reality technique which the poet uses is intended to show the gruesome experiences that the postcolonial peoples go through while postcolonial leadership continually gives the false impression to the outside world that everything is okay. Based on government propaganda, on the international front, Cameroon has often been referred to as a peaceful nation, but in reality the individual Cameroonian is living a traumatic nightmarish existence. This is what the poet represents in the metaphor of the forest as seen from outside and as experienced from inside. Little wonder therefore that Emmanuel Fru Doh says "Whether speaking softly or shouting as is typical of some of his poetic voices, the poems ... urge one to look closely at one's world in a bid to improve upon the oppressed lot of so many unacknowledged victims" (vi). Alembong manifests a sensitive artistic imagination and is keen to the immediate problems plaguing his society. He diagnoses these problems with the incisiveness of a seasoned bard and conveys them with the refreshing simplicity of communal wisdom:

> A forest is a jungle
> To those who see it from without;
> When in, we learn that

> The bamboo that tries to rub shoulders with the
> mahogany
> Will find it brought down by the wind.
>
> A forest is a jungle
> To those who see it from without;
> When in, we learn that
> The parrot will lose its eyes to the night
> Should it try to mimic the owl.
>
> A forest is a jungle
> To those who see it from without;
> When in, we learn that
> Bugs suck to live, not to kill,
> As bees sting to give, not to take. (2-3)

Although the first two lines of each stanza maintain the irregular refrain of defining what the forest is as expressed in the first four stanzas, the structure of the poem has changed both in terms of line number and thought. The last three stanzas are different in that they have five lines each instead of the four lines of the preceding stanzas. This increase in line length is accompanied by an increase in the level of wisdom that one gets from trying to understand the philosophy of the forest and everything about it. The emphasis is no longer on what "we see'; it has changed to what "we learn". The experience has moved from what is seen with the physical eyes to what is seen with the innate eyes – the lesson that is learned. This lesson makes up what is referred to earlier as the refreshing simplicity of communal wisdom embodied in proverbial language. The proverbs "The bamboo that tries to rub shoulders with the mahogany/Will find it brought down by the wind" and "The parrot will lose its eyes to the night/Should it try to mimic the owl" (2-3) in more general sense cautions people to recognize their individual potential – as bamboo and as mahogany, as parrot and as owl. In a more specific sense it indicts the Darwinian survivalist tendencies of politicians who are ready to destroy whoever attempts to measure up to the range of their power. Alembong understands the politics and poetics of existence in his context and so processes the ugliness of the truth about life in his society in insightful proverbialism.

Forest Echoes can be read as a metaphor of Cameroon's historical journey and the experiences that the people, especially those of Anglophone Cameroon, have gone through. Published in 2011 and republished almost immediately in 2012, *Forest Echoes* alongside other poetry texts like Oscar C. Labang's *My Country Took A Wrong Turn*, is a major artistic way of celebrating the 50th Anniversary of independence of Cameroon. The poems in the collection especially the title poem is a soulful cry for the people of Cameroon to look back at 50 years of existence as an independent nation and see what history we have made as a people.

Alembong's questions are similar to those Labang asks:

> What has fifty years of existence brought to the nation?
> This void of brine
> Where the wounds of History are repeatedly dipped...
> The sterile dragon helixes on the executive pew,
> With monstrous eyes and an abrasive voice
> (Labang, 2)

Labang's poem is an expressive appeal and also a passionate condemnation of the varied forces that have shaped and tilted the fortune of the nation towards the bad-fated rancour in which the people now wallow. Similarly, Alembong's poem is a livid lament about the journey to nationhood and how the people, especially Anglophones, found themselves in this situation. The anger is hardly perceived because the poem is dense with strong images and suggestive symbols. They convey, however, in every sense the poet's opinion about what history, greed, exploitation and neo-colonial leadership has done to the Cameroonian nation and Anglophones in particular. As Emmanuel Fru Doh rightly observes in the "Foreword" to the collection, "*Forest Echoes* displays an oeuvre which explores the painful and equally challenging double consciousness required and typical of an Anglophone-Cameroonian in an effort to establish and maintain his or her identity and sanity in Cameroon today" (vi). Going by what Poet, one of the speakers in the poem says at the beginning, the poem is a tale of the past and the present presented in such grandeur that the reader finds himself fixated by the refined poetic and linguistic twists. It opens in the typology of a traditional tale with Poet situating the setting and what is going on thus:

POET:
Wife's food still a-cooking
Son and daughter at arm's length –
Nailed to their bamboo stools,
Scourged by fetters of smoke
And the thirst for lore –
He chose to pass the time
In song and story:
The tale of old and new. (4)
...
POET:
Voice cleared –
The way our birds clear their throats
To sing the song of dawn, to make
Sleep leave our heads –
The tale hung on his lips, ripe for harvest
Like pointed breasts for sucking. (4)

The poem occupies two frames – that of a song as represented in the refrain performed by the Chorus, repetitive pattern of speech by Poet and Narrator, and other sonic devices spread in different parts of the poem. The other frame that the poem fits in is that of a story and what Poet says in the above excerpt gives a context for the story to be enacted. The children are sitting with their mother who is preparing food in the kitchen. Although the kitchen is stuffy with "fetters of smoke" the children seem determined "Nailed to their bamboo stools" to wait for the food. Like in a characteristic traditional setting the anonymous "He", probably the Narrator who will surface later in the poem, decides to tell a tale of the suffering of his people (Anglophones) in a union they thought was going to make them a better people since they were crossing the river to meet their brothers and friends. It is "The tale of old and new" suggesting the idea that it spans the history of the life of the speaker and his people. The next speech by Poet prepares the ground for Narrator to emerge and tell the tale. After situating the children, their mother and what they are doing the poet captures in expansive comparative terms the atmosphere outside as seen in the following beautiful lines that emphasize what is going on outside:

POET:
Outside,
The sky tore its garment open
And unleashed a dark fog over the land.
Outside,
Haunting phrases of wailing owls
Rescued the land to misery.
Outside,
The hen and the partridge passed for one another,
As the pig and the boar the same.

Outside,
Unshod feet smashed their homeward ways,
Embracing the fog like the hen her chicks.
Outside,
The land was enveloped like walnuts in their shells
And birds slept with their eyes open. (5)

The personification of the sky tearing its garment to release fog for the evening troposphere, and that of owls wailing ominous "phrases" as well as the images of the hen, partridge, pig and boar all create the scene of a typical village setting characterized by the charm and activity of all cosmic forces working in separate dimensions. In this poem, Alembong comes out as a poet to bear testimony to that which his people have been subjected to in the past and in the present. This is where Alembong puts on the vestment of the poet and comes out to speak, to sing and to preach to his people about their fate and what they must do to come to terms with themselves.

As the Poet recedes, the Narrator emerges. The Poet fits squarely in the personality of the Biblical John the Baptist as his job in the early part of the poem is to clear the way, define the path and clarify the bases on which the Rabi will speak. The Narrator therefore comes to focus only after the Poet has defined the context, situated the story, and announced what is going on inside and outside. And when the Narrator begins to speak, centrality in his first two speeches is given to river and water imagery "A river it was that lay between us" (6). The metaphor of the forest as a representation of Cameroon is suggested both by the river and the "us" – a reference to the River Mungo and the two parts of Cameroon respectively. The impression that is sent home from the first two speeches is that the river was a natural way of keeping these two parts separated; it was a natural boundary that was bridged by colonial greed "stranger-masters" and later separated by them thereby leaving the people to speak "in two tongues". The centrality of water is also evident in the fact that the poet associates "us" to the colonial master in terms of river imagery. He refers to the partition of Cameroon between France and Britain after the First World War thus "one went to the Seine for water / And the other, for true, to the Thames" (7). The Seine refers metaphorically to France and the Thames to Britain. Here water loses its universal power as an image of cleansing and is associated with separation, domination and exploitation. However, it retains its life-giving function.

In "Forest Echoes" the historicity of the journey of Cameroon through the years of struggle for independence and in its development as a nation through various stages is brought to focus. A major historical event which the poet looks back to with fervours of anger is the reunification of February 11, 1961. Perceived as a journey across the river, (supposedly the River Mungo), the Narrator in "Forest Echoes" laments the crossing and the betrayal that has followed the union between French Cameroun and British Southern Cameroons:

> *NARRATOR:*
> We crossed the river with our heads high,
> As high as baobab leaves that tower the forest.
> We crossed to meet our brothers, so we thought,
> And there it dawned on us that a brother's punch
> Is harder to bear than that of a stranger.
> We crossed to meet our friends, so we thought,
> And there it dawned on us that no one
> Counts the teeth in the mouth of a friend's dog.
> We crossed to form a great union, so we thought,
> And there it dawned on us that a wise man does not
> Measure his footprints with those of an elephant.
> (12)

There is the juxtaposition of expectation and failure as the narrator tries to come to terms with the reality that they encountered when they crossed the river. The hope of meeting their brothers and friends is ruined because they are not received with equal warmth. The proverbs in this part of the poem continually point to the fact that the narrator and his people did not take careful consideration before crossing the river to "form a great union"; they were excited by the necessity to reunite with the people they thought were their brothers. Butake has demonstrated in *Family Saga* that they are actually brothers but the problem is that one brother Kamala thinks that he is superior to Kamalo. The Narrator in the above excerpt is therefore typical of Kamala in a lament over the way his brother Kamalo treats him in a union that was supposed to be based on equality.

"Forest Echoes" is a loud and long cry from the heart of the forest (metaphor of Cameroon) performed by three personalities: "Poet", "Narrator" and "Chorus". The poem evokes the Anglophone problem in ways that are unique and fascinating and draws the attention of the reader to the core problems that continue to plague the nation. It is a carefully written poem, buried in folkloric qualities that summon elemental forces from all parts of the universe and generate proverbial wisdom to tell the story of how the nation and most particularly Anglophones found themselves here. Anglophone expectations at the time of the union are communicated in a chain of repetitions that emphasizes the reason for which they crossed and the contrary which they have encountered.

NARRATOR:
We crossed because of the urge to retrace our roots
Oblivious of the fact that it is on its old trail
That an animal meets its death.
For since we crossed
Our sun's face has turned grey.
Since we crossed
Our moon no longer appears at night.
Since we crossed

> Our sky has worn a black veil.
> Since we crossed
> Our birds no longer sing in different ways.
> Since we crossed
> Our seedlings have never seen the harvest sun.
> Since we crossed
> Our roads have become the ant's trail.
> Since we crossed
> Our farms have been seized by locusts. (13)

The expectations of the Anglophones were that they were going back to the condition from which they originated; they were going back to meet their brothers and friends but these expectations failed as suggested in the proverb "it is on its old trail that the animal meets its death" (13). The litany of images that follow this proverb typifies Anglophone fate in very glaring manners. The images that are used to express the fate of the Anglophones in the union are dominantly negative. The greyness of the "sun's face" and the fact that the moon no longer appears at night or that a "black veil" now covers the sky are signs of the decline of Anglophone fate. From such extra-terrestrial imagism the poet turns to terrestrial images like "birds", "seedlings", "roads" and "farms". On the Anglophone part of the country, the birds have lost the beauty of their chorus as they "no longer sing in different ways"(13); seedlings have failed to grow to ripe fruits; roads have been neglected to the point where they are reduced to mere "ant trails", and locusts (a symbol of greed and exploitation) have invaded their farms. The repetition "Since we crossed" is strategic in revealing the Narrator's sense of profound frustration. The frustration arises from the lack of unity and respect in the union. The type of unity and collaboration that Anglophones expected is expressed in more vivid terms in the poem "Song of Awambeh" in which a lady (suggestive of Anglophone Cameroon) bewails the fact that her co-wife is exploiting her in the compound of her husband. She cries out about the supposed unity:

> I agreed that you should enter this compound.
> A woman needs others
> To join in cooking for a man.
> To join in warming his bed,
> To join in giving him children,
> To join in feeding his pigs,
> To join in tethering his goats,
> To join in working on his cocoa farms,
> To join in working on his coffee farms,
> To join in working in his palm bushes.
> This is what our mothers tell us.
> This is what I was told
> The day I left for my husband's compound.
> This is what you were told
> The day you left for our husband's compound. (62)

The insistence on "To join" which is repeated multiple times in this stanza is meant to call the co-wife to consciousness of the fact that as two independent wives (like French Cameroun and Southern Cameroons) they are supposed to be collaborators without one trying to lord-over the other. The lamenting wife's complaints are akin to those of Anglophone Cameroonians who feel cheated, betrayed, and abandoned by their Francophone counterparts in the union they mutually agreed to create. Within this context, Alembong's marriage allegory in "Song of Awambeh" corroborates Victor Epie Ngome's allegorical play titled *What God Has Put Asunder* and Butake's family allegory *Family Saga*. Like these playwrights, Alembong's poem more closely to Ngome's play show the plight of a cheated woman in a marriage where they swore equality as co-wives. But more vindictive than Ngome's exploited character, Weka, the cheated Awambeh in Alembong's "Song of Awambeh" invokes elemental forces like the sun to be her witness and even curses the co-wife for feeding on the fruit of her labour – symptomatic of the exploitation of the natural resources of the English speaking part of Cameroon.

Written in the style of an African oral tale, with a chorus that participates in recalling the central issue, the poem through the voice of a Poet and later the Narrator traces the history of the people of Cameroon, pokes at some of the wounds of history and indict those who have ruined the nation to this point. The chorus has a particular refrain that it repeats all through the poem:

CHORUS:
    When will our streams flow to their cradle
    And leave the Seine to its stony ways?
    When will our fishes gather in the great pond
    And leave preying hawks to feast on fires?

The Chorus speaks in proverbial language making use of the image of streams that have to flow back to their own source and fishes that should assemble in their own ponds. This is suggestive of the complete independence that the previously colonial nations should have. The Chorus is suggesting that Cameroon and other formerly colonized people should completely severe links with the colonial masters seen in the image of the "Seine" and the "preying hawks". It is worthy of note that both the "Seine" and the "hawks" have negative attributes "stony ways" and "preying" respectively, and these reveal the negative effect of western powers on the colonized peoples or nations.

    Hallmarks of Alembong's poetry are the linguistic simplicity made sophisticated by a strong imagistic pattern and proverbial wisdom. As an oralist, Alembong in his poetry expresses a sincere passion for communal wisdom and storytelling through the traditional oral bard. While the role of this wise-bard figure comes out most glaringly in "Forest Echoes", other poems in this rich repertoire bears convincing evidence that this is a poet well groomed and well-grounded in the ways of his people. The title of the collection *Forest Echoes* gives centrality to the image of the forest and the first three poems build on this image to represent the different experiences of the Cameroon nation.

CHAPTER THREE
APOCALYPTIC NATIONALISM: DESTRUCTION AND REBIRTH IN SAMPSON NKWETATANG'S "MALEDICTION UPON THE WICKED"

This chapter analyses the poetry of Sampson Nkwetatang within the framework of apocalyptic literature. Poetry to Sampson Nkwetatang is an instrument with multiple functions but the most visible and recurrent function of that instrument is to curse those who have ruined the postcolonial Cameroon nation and to offer a supplication for God to intervene on behalf of the helpless people subjected to different and multiple forms of misery. This chapter is based on the premise that in "Malediction Upon the Wicked *(Who Have Ruined Cameroon)*", Nkwetatang comes out forcefully and convincingly as an apocalyptic voice announcing doom and seeking salvation or rebirth for the postcolonial Cameroon nation. The poem can comfortably be classified as apocalyptic literature, which has been defined by Adela Yarbro Collins as:

> a genre of revelatory literature with a narrative framework in which a revelation is mediated by another worldly being to a human recipient,

> disclosing a transcendent reality which is both temporal, insofar as it envisages eschatological salvation, and spatial, insofar as it involves another, supernatural world. (Collins, 62)

Like the biblical John, the revelator, Sampson Nkwetatang's poet-prophet is strongly opposed to and alienated from the existing social and political order in Cameroon. The poet is an irremediable exile without necessarily living out of his homeland. His condition of exile is that which Shara McCallum describes as "a psychic condition that many writers... seem to share: a feeling of being apart from others in our community and even from ourselves, whether at home or abroad" (McCallum, Par. 22)[vii]. The poet-prophet stands at a distance, at the "summit of the Western High Plateau" (Nkwetatang, 28), - like John in the island of Patmos - and pronounces destruction and condemnation on the political power structure as well as predicts the overthrow of the corrupt regime in the postcolonial Cameroon nation.

"Malediction Upon the Wicked" is a typified example of postcolonial apocalypse or apocalyptic nationalism which Teresia Heffernan describes as a point in modern apocalypse "where the emergence of the nation is understood as the point of arrival for an 'imagined community'" (Heffernan). Postcolonial apocalypse or the apocalypse of liberation to use the broad term is one form of postmodern apocalypse especially given the fact that it is entirely the product of human action and not a divine prophecy, and that it seeks to liberate postcolonial peoples both from neo-colonial West and from postcolonial dictatorships. The twentieth century according to James Berger has been "thoroughly marked, perhaps even defined by, apocalyptic impulses, fears representations and events" (388). In situating what is postmodern apocalypse, Berger outlines four principal forms of post war apocalyptic representation: "The first is nuclear war, the second is the Holocaust, the third is the apocalypses of liberation (feminist, African American, postcolonial) and the fourth is what is loosely called 'postmodernity'" (Berger, 390). Nkwetatang's "Malediction" can be categorized in the third form "apocalypse of liberation" because it communicates "some revelatory catastrophe whose traumatic force reshapes all that preceded it and all that follows" (Berger, 392). The people that moved through revolution from the old colonial nation imagining a radically new postcolonial nation are faced with the problems of ruin and are contemplating another new nation – a post-postcolonial nation. This is the basis of apocalyptic nationalism.

Nkwetatang's "Malediction Upon the Wicked" can be divided into three movements of thought or visionary experiences. The First Vision evokes bleak images of the condition of the present day postcolonial Cameroonian nation and shows the levels of catastrophic horror that the nation and its people are experiencing. The dominant symbolism shows a nation in complete collapse and the people are in a state of despair, oppression and misery. Typical of most Apocalypses Nkwetatang's "Malediction Upon the Wicked" is written from a context of oppression, persecution and despair. The poet contextualizes the poem and sets it in the midst of catastrophic changes in postcolonial Cameroon. He shows that the previously well-ordered nation and nationalistic views are in collapse. As an apocalyptic writer, Nkwetatang situates his speaker in the midst of the catastrophic destruction of the way of life in the postcolonial Cameroon nation.

The poem opens with a declaration of doom and despair resulting from the activities of Cameroonians who have ruined the nation. The prophet figure in the poem is a nationalist similar in character to Ntungwukuye in John Ngongkum Ngong's *Chants of a Lunatic*. Ntungwukuye is a multifaceted and multi-visionary prophet who is burdened by the problems of his nation and when he tries to speak against the grossly unjust system he is regarded as a hare-brained. Unlike Ntungwukuye who submits to the follies of his people by allowing them to define him, the unnamed prophet in Nkwetatang's "Malediction Upon the Wicked" distances himself to the hilly plateaus and from there he pronounces destruction as well as supplicates for renewal. The message communicated is the aspiration of the underprivileged, those who have been pushed by the power elite to the margins of society, about the nation. Heffernan argues that "apocalyptic writings about the nation also express the dreams of the ostracized and the oppressed about the renewal or rebirth of a community" (Heffernan, Par. 3). For the rebirth to take place, or for the dream community to come into being, there must be the destruction of the old order, which in the case of the poem under study is the present Cameroonian national status-quo and socio-political system.

In this apocalyptic tradition, "Malediction Upon the Wicked" "challenges the established order, confuses accepted rules, and ignores the prevalent codes of reason" (Heffernan, Par. 3), as it opens with a message of doom and progresses to prophesies of destruction and renewal. Although the nation is blessed with natural resources that span across its borders, ruin has been declared upon it. "O' Cameroon thou cradle of our fathers, / Blessed nation with pleasant waters ... / Beloved nation with evergreen forest..., ruin is your portion" (Nkwetatang, 28). The doom which the poet-prophet announces results from the activities of the very sons and daughters of the nation. The condemnation here is similar to that of Jeremiah on the nation of Judah for their sins and their faithlessness (Chapters 1-10). The ruling class is responsible for the oppression and despair that has taken hold of the nation. The speaker assumes the position of the alienated prophet speaking strange fates to the people of Cameroon. He cries out: "Your sons and daughters have put you to shambles. /They have sold you to the highest bidders. /They have shepherded you into the dungeon" ((Nkwetatang, 27). The poet-prophet addresses the nation directly, talking to it as though it is human and can understand the evil that has taken hold of life or the ruin that has been brought unto it by its children. The direct address to the nation especially in the line "They have smoked you to suffocation. / They have strangled you to death /And they have lowered you a thousand feet beneath the earth's surface" (Nkwetatang, 27), transfers human agencies to the nation and confirms the general tendency of attributing qualities of a mother or father to the nation in postcolonial Africa. In the case of Cameroon the nation is generally referred to as "Fatherland" whereas other postcolonial nations are referred to as "Motherland". Thus, the "Fatherland" has been brought to ruin and the degree of destruction is compared to strangulation, death and burial. The diction is categorical in its declaration and definition of the ruin. The nation has been destroyed "shambles" and "sold to…the highest bidders" (Nkwetatang, 27). The images of "suffocation" and "death" show the level of ruin that has befallen the nation. In apocalyptic literature of nationalism, the hope is that the death and burial of the present nation will give rise to a new nation with a more profound sense of communal existence.

The message of destruction is sustained or re-echoed in other parts of the poem but there is a shift from the general idea to the destruction of the ecosystem and the economy. The nation has thus been subjected to multiple forms of destruction or every facet of the nation is feeling the power of evil and destruction. The nation is humanized in a more direct way when the speaker uses endearments saying:

> Dear fatherland thy worth no tongue can tell,
> today, you are exposed to the ravening sun.
> Your fertile farmlands are barren.
> Your streets are packed with unemployed young
> boys and girls craving for livelihood in vain.
> Your forests are infested with foreign exploiters
> who export your wood at no profit to you.
> Your currency has been flown overseas and kept in
> banks which pay no interest to you.
> Your economy has been trodden to ground level.
>
> (Nkwetatang, 27)

The exposure to the "ravening sun", and barrenness of lands that were once fertile are indications of the change in the fortune of the nation. There is dualism that is characteristic of apocalypse but this dualism does not show the present condition and the possible future condition as in the normal apocalypse. Rather, it shows the level of despair and destruction – the past 'beauty' and the present decay that the nation is going through. It has moved from a condition of normalcy to an abnormal state of affairs and the poet-prophet in the poem is lamenting this change because it has brought doom and destruction to the nation. The poem makes subtle reference to the issue of domination and oppression by foreign powers that are partly responsible for the hardship in the nation. Another level of destruction that the nation is experiencing is capital flight which has led to the crumbling of the economy and high unemployment. The youth are "craving for livelihood in vain" (Nkwetatang, 27) because of unemployment.

There is logical declaration of destruction and despair in the poem. From a general prophecy of ruin, through the levels of destruction that the nation has experienced, the prophecy shift to the destruction of the ecology and how the nation's fertile lands have become deserts because the "forest are infested with foreign exploiters" (Nkwetatang, 27). The human condition takes centre stage in the fifth stanza. In the following stanza, the subject of destruction and despair shifts again from the ecological destruction to human misery, pain, and frustration all of which are conditions necessary for an apocalypse. The poet cries out:

> Your children are leading the most miserable lives
> ever known to humanity.
> They rise in the early morning and stare at the
> future with sunken eyes
> like vultures staring at the aridity of the wilderness.
> They sojourn from one region to another in search
> of daily bread like nomads on transhumance.
> They cry out in childbirth pains but nobody attends
> to them.
> They shout to the top of their voices but nobody
> hearkens to them.
>
> Theirs is hunger and thirst.
> Theirs is pain and chagrin.
> Theirs is misery and woe.
> Theirs is destitution and death.
>
> (Nkwetatang, 27-8)

Sampson in this stanza assumes the position of a divine intercessor that has appeared to interpret the visions of horror that postcolonial Cameroon is going through; he reveals secret knowledge about the condition of the nation and its people. The poem is the product of hard times and the poet-prophet speaks to the Cameroonian people as they struggle to come to terms with the plight in which they find themselves. The short four-line stanza above is characteristic in the way it defines the deplorable condition of the people. The anaphoric device gives particular expressiveness as it both intensifies the profundity of despair and gives even greater relevance to the apocalyptic message. The repetition of "Theirs is" gives equal profundity to "hunger and thirst", "pain and chagrin", "misery and woe" and "destitution and death" (Nkwetatang, 28). In the first vision, the poet-prophet speaks in a manner similar to that of the Prophet Isaiah. In the first 39 Chapters, Isaiah points out the sins of the North and South Kingdoms before declaring severe punishment to them and the neighbouring nations. This replication of the prophetic pattern of Isaiah gives additional impetus to the apocalyptic undertones of the poem.

    The first six stanzas of the poem convey the message of despair and destruction that typifies existence in the nation because of the ruinous activities of the people. It creates the apocalyptic context of oppression, persecution and despair, and shows the various levels through which the nation is experiencing these. This is followed by the second vision in which there is the pronouncement of judgement. The poet-prophet comes out strongly and passes sentence on "whoever" is responsible for the present state of the nation. At this level Nkwetatang situates himself as the boundary between the world and the word, and envisions the power of the spoken word as the instrument for the destruction of the perpetrators of evil. He speaks out:

> Be him son, be her daughter of this nation of
>   whatever age, of whatever tribe

> and of whatever social standing, born of the womb
> of a woman, fed with her breasts
> and given infant upbringing on her laps who has
> contributed
> in one way or the other in ruining this nation,
> malediction upon him or her today for, this is the
> day of reckoning. (Nkwetatang, 28)

The target of destruction as defined here is not necessarily the power elite or ruling class. Malediction is on anyone who has contributed in any way to make the nation what it is at the moment the speaker is talking. Any individual who has natural birth and upbringing and that has contributed to the corruption of the nation shares in the curse that the prophet pronounces. The prophet seems to be conscious of the fact that the present state of chaos, misery and frustration could be the work of a divine force. However, he is well aware that it is the work of Cameroonians. The destruction of the nation is not a divine act; the citizens of the nation are responsible for it. This is typical of postmodern apocalypse – it is man-made. The complete destruction of the forces of evil that have ruined the nation is what the prophet seeks as he pronounces:

> At the summit of the Western High Plateau,
> I stand and pronounce the peril of the wicked who
> have ruined this blessed nation.
> I lift my hands to heaven and call upon the
> Almighty God

> to send down devastating fireworks and consume them. (Nkwetatang, 28)

In this revolutionary poetic prophesy, Nkwetatang stands as the consciousness of the collective. From the heights of the "Western High Plateau" the poet passes judgment on the nation and its people. The speaker seems to have reached the peak of apocalyptic doom. He has little or even no faith in the potential of his people to save their country. He has come to that realization that human endeavour leaves very little possibility for progress or positive development; that things as they look are bad and they are only going to get worse as far as men remain in control of the fate of the nation. He therefore turns to transcendental forces for assistance: "Lord, stretch them to breaking point. /Put insurmountable barricades against their diabolic maltreatment of peace-loving peoples… We count on you and on no one else" (Nkwetatang, 28). The recourse to God gives a peculiar apocalyptic turn to the poem as it becomes an on-going conflict between God and Satan, or good and evil and the speaker himself is powerless in the face of growing evil. He represents the collective unconscious of the marginalized portion of his nation and declares their reliance on God to destroy the ever increasing evil of his society. This message resonates in another of Nkwetatang's poem "Lord, Save Cameroon from Shackles" in which he cries out to the Almighty:

> Lord, save Cameroon from shackles,
> For political tycoons want to make her their treasure hunt.
> Long, long have her children suffered from physical and mental torture
> Resulting from prolonged economic depression, massive unemployment
> And both active service and shameful retirement frustration to the dead.
> Long, long have they requested for the betterment of their lives to no hearing. (Nkwetatang, 32)

The entire poem, like the first stanza, constitutes a passionate and fervent call on God to intervene and disrupt the plans of destruction that "political tycoons" have mapped for the nation. In the apocalyptic tradition, the poet is beseeching God to intervene in the present day condition of Cameroon "Cameroon deserves to be more than what she is today" (Nkwetatang 33). The "today" or the now is the focus of apocalyptic pronouncements and Nkwetatang's persona in "Lord, Save Cameroon from Shackles" is concerned with the moment he is speaking because he has realised that although Cameroon is the "richest nation on earth", postcolonial leadership has reduced it to muddles.

The poet makes an endeavour to show God the disparities that exist between the rulers of the nation who are perceived as the evil forces and the people. Those who represent evil or who have ruined the nation are living in luxury whereas the rest of the population is living in wretched conditions.

> Lord, these our sons and daughters have caused us irreparable damages.
> We live in dilapidated ghettoes while they live in great mansions.
> We trek while they pull in provocatively expensive cars.
> We languish in abject poverty while they float on stupendous riches.
> We cry out in pains of circumcision; they laugh in banquets of champagne.
> The wealth they enjoy belongs to us all; they sit on it either by crook or crank. (Nkwetatang, 28-29)

The binarism created here is strategic in defining the two camps that are involved in this historical struggle – the "we" and the "they"; the haves and the have-nots, the ruling elite and the masses. The ruling elite has violated the social contract and according to Carole Pateman "The social contract is the point of origin, or birth, of civil society" (115). The point where the social contract does not operate is the point the society becomes uncivil and therefore needs a rebirth, which the poet-prophet seeks to achieve by declaring an end to the present corrupt social and political order. It is the point where according to Karl Marx "the political liberators [of anti-colonial nationalism] reduce citizenship, the *political community,* to a mere *means"* (Marx, 43) of achieving their private rather than public visions for the nation. These forces in apocalyptic frames represent the forces of good and evil that are constantly conflicting. By drawing attention to the various forms of marginalization and oppression when addressing the "Lord", the poet is giving concrete reason to the Lord to punish or destroy these leaders.

The poet-prophet embodies the consciousness of the new nation as he tries to reorder the structures in a bid to attain meaning and ensure continuity in his community. When the voice refers to those who are ruining the nation as "our sons and daughters", the reader gets an indication that the poet-prophet is an old man, probably one who has seen the evolution of the nation from its point of inception to the present stage and so thinks that rebirth and renewal is the precondition for continuous existence. Although the speaker in postcolonial and modern apocalypse is no longer a biblical figure, it is still written in the "name of a famous figure of the past" and is made to meet "a need for the people's continued communication with their God" (Harris, 179). Interestingly, the poet-speaker still shows a sense of affinity with the agents of evil and destruction. However, he does not share in their evil and greedy vision. His intension in referring to them as "our sons and daughters" is to show that the very people who have wrecked the state are part of its progeny. The notion of irreparable damage also points to the fact that human capacity cannot redeem the damage done to the nation; divine or supernatural intervention is absolutely necessary.

Although the postcolonial nation suffers some form of foreign domination (in the form of neo-colonialism) as is usually the case in apocalyptic literature in general, in postcolonial apocalypse the forces of domination usually originate from within the nation in the form of (bad) leadership. The form of leadership is so evil that every possible legitimate means of getting it off the realm of power has failed "Neither through the ballot box nor voluntarily are they willing to leave / power for others to try their turn" (Nkwetatang, 29). The struggle of the people to bring sanity and to ask for their rights is marred with further destruction and murder "In our desperate attempt to request for transparency and good governance, / we have lost many of our brothers and sisters gunned down / by conscienceless men in cavalry boots" (Nkwetatang, 29). The domination and destruction of postcolonial nations is the handiwork of western neo-colonialism as it is the handiwork of postcolonial African leadership. After showing the disparities between the ruling elite and the masses and telling the Lord how these people have clung to power with a strong will never to leave, the poet-prophet beseeches the Lord to destroy the wicked: "Lord, pursue the wicked who have put this blessed nation asunder" and "Lord, declare war upon those who have put this country to shambles" (Nkwetatang, 29). Nkwetatang's prophetic declaration of the end of the regime aligns with Bate Besong's equally strong declaration of doom and destruction on the present political system that has ruined the nation. In "The Party's Over" Bate Besong celebrates the end of the tyranny of President Amadou Ahidjo's regime:

> Long we have listened to the howl of human misery
> The dying voices from that human world below:
> Filling the gaps
> Of the distant exultations [...]
>
> Ah! In those days there was fear
> Booming loud and long in every skull
> We thought you and I;
> That it would always be like this. (15)

When Bate Besong say in the last two lines above that "We thought you and I / That it would always be like this" what he does not say, which is even more prophetic and revelatory, is that 'it would NOT always be like this'. This suggests the end of long years of "human misery", of "dying voices" and of "fear" which haunts the imagination of the people. It also suggests the end of the tyrant and dictator that orchestrates this horrifying existential condition. Besong and Nkwetatang thus share a close affinity in their prophetic pronouncements of the end of the regime. They also share in the idea of hope that the horror that the nation is experiencing will come to an end.

In the third vision, Nkwetatang engages in a call for God to intervene not just to punish the committers of evil as he does in some parts of the second vision. This is the poet's final vision and it ends with a plea for God to bring the present state of affairs to What John Carter in discussing the characteristic of apocalyptic literature calls "a cataclysmic end and establishing a better situation" (Carter, 4). His particular focus is on the intervention of God to declare victory over the forces of evil and to cleanse Cameroon. This is a primary function of apocalyptic literature as it is built on the belief that God will intervene to bring the evil of the world to an end and proclaim His ultimate victory. From this premise Nkwetatang cries out for a redemptive cleansing of the postcolonial Cameroon nation:

> Lord, we wish this nation is cleansed.
> We wish it is delivered from the hands of Lucifer's altar boys and girls.
> It is our fervent wish to see the dawn of a new era.
> ....
> An era void of manipulations of unpopular opinion in favour of selfish interests.

The poet reinforces the wish of his people when he cries out to the Lord "Indeed, we wish to see an era of the worship of wisdom, of human kindness / and of the wellbeing of all and sundry..." (Nkwetatang, 29). The new nation which the poet envisions is one that gives value to every individual in the nation; it is one that makes the individual to have a feeling of belonging and worth in his nation. The worship of wisdom is important in such a nation because it is fundamental to the understanding that the nation is a community that should uphold public values not private egoistic values as those practiced by the present leadership. The speaker is talking about a post-rupture nation, better still a post-postcolonial nation because the postcolonial or anti-colonial nation has failed. In the post-postcolonial nation, the margins that are used to divide the people into ruling elite and subalterns will be dissolved. The post-postcolonial nation "envisions the eradication of margins and the closing of gaps in the formation of a community that emerges at the end of history; cutting across class, race, language, and gender boundaries, a national boundary circumscribes differences" (Heffernan, Par. 6).

There is profuse use of biblical allusion in the third or final vision as the poet-prophet continually invokes different images to tear down the current corrupt system and replace it with the new vision of the nation. In requesting the Lord to destroy those who have ruined Cameroon the speaker says "Outmatch them like Jesus who outmatched Satan for forty days and nights" (Nkwetatang, 30). There are also references to the destruction of Sodom and Gomorrah, the plagues on King Pharaoh of Egypt, and the "unclean in the time of Noah" (Nkwetatang, 29-30). It is worthy of note that these images and biblical references all relate to the idea of destruction. Sodom and Gomorrah was destroyed because sexual evil had taken hold of the city and there was need for rebirth. The plagues that came upon the people of Egypt were intended to show the power of God to Pharaoh so that he may release the people of Israel from slavery. The people of Israel encountered a new birth and a new nation after the plagues caused King Pharaoh to release them and allow them to go out of Egypt. The unclean at the time of Noah caused the destruction of the earth and the beginning of a 'new' creation, the rebirth of a new nation from the family of Noah. Reference to these images therefore are effective because the all draw attention to the destruction that the poet-prophet is prophesying, he continually evokes images of destruction to suggest that the present Cameroonian nation is not different from the nation of Sodom and Gomorrah or the nation of Egypt or the biblical nation in the time of Noah. These nations share a common denominator – they are dominated by different forms of evil. Like these nations, the speaker thinks that the Cameroon nation has been overcome by evil and so needs to be destroyed and a new nation born in its place. This destruction needs to be performed by someone that is stronger than the speaker – either the Lord himself or someone "Lord, if you will not come, please, send someone." (30).The speaker is a sage who understands the model and functioning of intercessory prayer. After invoking the Lord and insisting that he comes to the aid of his nation, the speaker challenges God by drawing again from the bible "And your word does not go and return unfulfilled..." / "This beloved nation counts on your rapid intervention to redeem this deplorable state of affairs." (30). The poet makes reference to the Book of Isaiah particularly to Chapter 55, where Isaiah is extending an invitation to thirty and says at some point "So shall my word be that goes forth out of my mouth: it shall not return unto me void, but it shall accomplish that which I please, and it shall prosper in the thing for which I sent it" (Verse 11). The poet-prophet is challenging God to fulfil his promise, which according to him is to bring relief to the Cameroon nation because its people have suffered enough afflictions in the hands of bad leaders. The poem ends more or less like the prophecies of Isaiah. The third vision sounds more like Chapters 56-66 of the Book of Isaiah in which Isaiah writes of the new Heavens and Earth - "For behold, I create new heavens and a new earth; and the former things will not be remembered or come to mind" (Chapter 65:17). The poet-prophet proclaims hope for the afflicted and judgment for the evil like

Isaiah did to the people of Israel during their days of affliction.

The poet-prophet blends history and narrative through the allusive device of using lines of direct quotes from the Cameroon National Anthem – another sign of apocalyptic nationalism. The first line of the first stanza "O' Cameroon thou cradle of our fathers," is coincidentally the first line of the National Anthem. By addressing the nation directly, the poet-prophet creates a filial link with the nation and gives greater possibility for his lamentation and prophecies to be authentic. Also, by addressing the "cradle" and invoking "our fathers" at the very beginning of the poem, the poet-prophet situates himself in-between history and narrative and so dissolves all possibilities of margins thereby making the poem a "narrative of the modern nation [which] envisions the eradication of margins and the closing of gaps in the formation of a community that emerges at the end of history; cutting across class, race, language, and gender boundaries" (Heffernan, Par. 6). This is because as Heffernan states "a national boundary circumscribes differences" (Par. 6). Only a nation without boundaries can share a real sense of community. Cameroon was, in the opinion of the poet-prophet, once such a nation "fatherland thy worth no tongue can tell" (Stanza 3). But the present condition is so horrible and bizarre that the poet thinks there is need for a rebirth of the nation.

In placing himself between narrative and history, Nkwetatang fulfils a fundamental function of apocalyptic writers because to them history becomes the visionary experience of the author. It is common knowledge that postcolonial Cameroon is beset by all forms of difficulty and crises, and writers have addressed these problems differently. But defining the problems in terms of apocalypse as Nkwetatang does in "Malediction Upon the Wicked" is uncommon. The problems of the postcolonial nation become in the hands of the poet severe vision of the fate and future of the people as they engage in the daily struggle of life "the past course of history as known to the actual author is made a prediction in the mouth of the purported author" (Martin Franzmann, 28). This is what Nkwetatang does in "Malediction" and like most apocalypses it is invested in the wisdom of an older person. In the opinion of the apocalyptic poet, all the indecencies of the present society must be eradicated for a perfectly "imagined community" as defined by Anderson to be attained. The poet therefore is an agent of destruction and reconstruction as he perceives a new community born from the ashes of the present corrupt postcolonial nation.

CHAPTER FOUR
LEADERSHIP FAILURE IN POSTCOLONIAL AFRICA: NYAA HANS NDAH'S *MY AFRICA*

When the venerable Nigerian pundit, Chinua Achebe, diagnosed the illness in the Nigerian society and professed that the trouble with Nigeria is the failure of leadership - because with good leaders Nigeria could resolve its inherent problems - he stated a fact that is verifiable and true not only to the case of Nigeria but to Africa of then and now as a whole. The crisis of leadership is a central concern in much of Cameroon poetry in English and a major theme in Nyaa Hans Ndah's poetry as expressed in *My Africa*. Ndah criticizes the power structure through imaginative creative patterns that project and reveal the ills of the ruling elite and how this cripples the nation. According to Shadrach Ambanasom, the "criticism of public officers is but an indirect advocacy of good governance, of economic and political transparency in the management of public affairs" (2).

Leadership theoreticians have theorized the term "Leadership" in many ways. Despite the variance in thought and definition of leadership, scholars in the field agree on a number of components which can be combined to give a clear and agreeable definition to the word. Peter Northhouse in *Leadership: Theory and Practice* defines leadership as "a process whereby an individual influences a group of individuals to achieve a common goal" (3). This definition is relevant in the context of this paper because it raises the basic components of leadership, which are apparently absent when one examines the leadership situation of postcolonial Africa whether from a political perspective, leadership context or literary interpretation. This definition is also relevant because it takes away the possibility of limiting leadership to the Head of States. As a "process", leadership "becomes available to everyone" and not just the designated leader of the group/nations (Northouse, 3).

While leadership is complex to define, leadership failure is even more complex to describe because of the subjective meanings that arise from the contexts and expectations of the audience. In the context of this analysis, leadership failure deals with the inability of the leader or leaders to make decisions that are consistent with the goals of the group thereby resulting in the lack of influence. It deals with what Mitchel and Scott refer to as "the crisis of political leadership" (445). One of the consequences of failure in public leadership is the lack of trust, which affects the leader's ability to influence the people. In the context of Africa, the picture of contemporary African leadership shows a clear scene of persistent and consistent failure in leadership. The goals of the African nations at the time of independence were to build societies based on freedom, respect, unity and equality because under the colonial regimes they were treated more as lesser beings. The activities of the leaders reveal an agenda that is contrary to the goals of these nations. There is the dominant absence of criteria such as "expertise, entrepreneurship and stewardship" (Langer, 446). Through an exegesis of selected poems from Nyaa Hans Ndah's collection, the analyses reveals the various dimensions of crises in leadership in postcolonial Africa; the various perspectives from which African leaders fail to meet up with the expectations of their citizens.

A major problem that plagues postcolonial African nations is the inability of leaders to give up power legitimately and legally. This problem which is at the centre of much of the wars and conflicts around Africa results from the absence of a democratic means of power transition. The poet is of the opinion that Africa's leaders cannot value and accept democracy because they are power hungry and corrupt. The welcoming of democracy is thus a question of guessing as the poet says in "Perhaps Democracy Cometh in the Morning When…" (36). The dependence on possibility is revealed through the use of the word "perhaps" – an expression of possibility with uncertainty. The coming of democracy is associated with the coming of joy "Perhaps joy cometh next morning / Like mature plant in Africa do now!" (36). The poet's hope is that the joy or beauty of democracy will be enjoyed by Africans when the present landscape of dictatorial regimes has died out. In the second wave of probability, the poet guesses that it is only with the empowerment of young people "the shoots of today" that democratic government can be fully established in Africa. The use of "perhaps" is very strategic in the poem and in the expression of the poet's belief. Ndah is expressing cautious optimism by making his opinion less definite about the implementation of democracy.

There is the expression of belief in the potential of youths to bring about democracy. He thinks that unlike the "mature plants", that is present leadership, the youths "will not cling dictatorially to power" (36). The poet is categorical in his thought about the potential of African youth to take the continent to a more practical and democratic condition. Unlike his opinion about the possible implementation of democracy which is expressed with scepticism, the idea about democracy being instituted by African youth is expressed with a degree of certainty "will not cling"; "will" used to state what is true or possible in a particular case or to state what is generally true. The yet-to-be-answered question is whether this is just another poetic act of wishful thinking or an imaginative act of prophecy or empirically tested truth.

Ndah thinks that death is the indisputable end for dictators. When the present generation of dictators have aged out and subjected themselves to the unbeatable will of death, Africa will then witness the advent of real democracy: "When they at last sleep eternally on the throne,/Perhaps "D" cometh in the morning" (36). The poet euphemizes the death of African dictators by referring to it as eternal sleep. This is an indication that he does not wish for a violent and catastrophic death as is usually the case. The death of the dictator will be marked by the burning of the throne. This act of burning the old throne symbolically marks not only the end of dictatorship and a break away from it but some sort of purification especially as we will "pray God to pardon them". The making of a new throne and the building of a new palace is suggestive of a new beginning during which African youths must "strive for pure democracy not for belly politics". This is a new vision of African leadership, not characterised by selfish individualism but by collective will to build the nation. It is only in such a situation that the "precious 'D'" will be acclaimed.

The idea of death as an ultimate end to dictatorship is also expressed in Dzekashu MacViban's "Comfortless Memories", a 2005 poem inspired by the death of the Togolese president Gnassingbe Eyadema.

Eyadema is a typical example of the tyranny that MacViban castigates in the poem. He is also a representative of the generation of dictators that Ndah thinks that will leave power either by yielding to the democratic wind or by death. Eyadema installed himself as president on 14 April 1967, after staging a successful military coup against then president Nicolas Grunitzky. He was also Minister of National Defense showcasing the desire of the tyrant to consolidate power in every way. This is what MacViban describes "Coup D'états in Africa" as the phenomenon whereby "A young snake kills its mother / Yet, it ain't different" (23). The overthrow of Grunitzky by Eyadema is not intended to improve on the condition of the Togolese people because the latter is not different from the former. Like most other African dictators, Eyadema had an extensive personality cult and survived several assassination attempts but as the poets say he could not escape the wheel of time. On February 5, 2005, he died of heart attack in a plane on transit as he was being evacuated for emergency treatment abroad. At the time of his death he was the longest-serving head of state in Africa. MacViban sees the death of Eyadema as an indication to African dictators that there is a more powerful force that they cannot, no matter what, overcome or escape its overpowering presence.

Dzekashu MacViban is concerned not so much with the fall of one tyrant; the focus of his philosophising is captured in the question in which he asks about the next fall. Like Nyaa who perceives the death of the dictator as "sleep", MacViban sees the death of the tyrant in terms of violent or disastrous crash. He perceives of it as a fall, which is somewhat more communicative in terms of intensity and effect compared to "sleep". Sleep is too comfortable a term to be associated to leaders who have caused the degree of pain and frustration for their people. Fall, which implies, to drop down from a higher level to a lower level, is more evocative of the suddenness of the collapse. He captures the natural end of the tyrant:

> Tyrants and sycophants sit with comfortless memories
> Perturbed by past, illegal and gory glories
>
> Their future reserves nothing but gloom
> Unlike their bygone days of bloom
>
> The wheel turns, causing many a great fall
> Togo has seen a fall – (27)

According to the poet, the tyrant is nervous and distressed by the very things he has done in the course of power. This is evoked in the very title of the poem "Comfortless Memories", which suggests a state of psychological discomfort. Their reflection on activities from their past, or their ability to remember things, is crowded by scenes of illegalities, and gruesome events. The poet combines two words with opposite connotations in the phrase "gory glories" to express the ironic use of power by African leaders. The oxymoron expressed in "gory glories" communicates the misuse and abuse of power in a vivid way. It reveals the fact that African leaders count their achievement only in terms of the unpleasant things they have done during their reign. The glory or special cause for pride, respect or pleasure is evident in the vast panorama of blood and violence that these tyrants cause for their nations.

It is possibly for the above reason that the poet thinks the end these leaders expect is an unpleasant one. For the leaders, "Their future reserves nothing but gloom / Unlike their bygone days of bloom" (MacViban, 24). Besides the oxymoron, the rhyming couplets also play a major role in expressing the condition of the leader and the fate that awaits them. Their memories are filled with scenes of "gory glories" as they move from their days of "bloom" to the day of "doom" which will mark their "fall". The repetition of "fall" and its association with the turning wheel (the natural passage of time) point to the contingency of the end of tyranny. Like Sany Abacha of Nigeria, Eyadema of Togo died of heart attack. MacViban seems to be pointing to the fact that heart attack for tyrants is the consequence of long days spent in unpleasant memories of the disaster they have perpetrated on their citizens. Ndah and MacViban are of the opinion that even when the citizens of these postcolonial nations cannot overthrow these leaders in fulfilment of the social contract as described by John Lock or if because of the personality cult of the leaders the citizens are not "justified in resisting the authority of a civil government" (Friend Celeste), nature or the passage of time will inevitably destroy them.

Ndah's meditation over the lack of democracy in Africa leads to agony, pain and frustration. He agonizes over the absence of democracy which is being blocked by African leaders. The imagination of the poet continually considers the possibilities of a democratic Africa but is disappointed each time. He writes:

> When over African politics I ponder,
> My wanders bleed anew.
> Many a day I ask why
> The winds of democracy are still
> Not breezing this way.
> Our leaders seem chasing away this cool wind
> That we badly need this way
> Dictatorship their choicest meal. (8)

The poet's source of agony is the dictatorial regimes that he sees all over the continent, and which are responsible for the undemocratic situation. He wonders why the ideals of democracy do not triumph in Africa where it is badly needed. He concludes, somewhat doubtfully, that it is being chased away by the leaders because "dictatorship is their choicest meal" (8). The poet is drowned into further worry when he realises that in other parts of the world democracy is an acceptable and practicable ideology. He says:

> When I gaze how manfully,
> Folks abroad absorb the democratic wind.
> I sweep down in worry and bellow
> Why this indispensable wind can't welcome?

The knowledge of the fact that in other continents – "abroad" people enjoy democratic privileges causes the speaker more distress. To him democracy is an indispensable value and so he wonders why in Africa we cannot welcome it. The absence of democracy is a subject that is also echoed in Oscar C. Labang's *This is Bonamoussadi* in which the poet describes democracy as a double headed snake.

Another problem with postcolonial African nations which surfaces in Ndah's poetry is that of dependence – the fact that African countries are not yet independent. The over-dependence of African countries on the colonial powers can be explained in part through Warren Bennis's "seven ages" of leadership (48). At the dawn of independence, African leaders were considered to be at the first stage of Bennis's stages – "infant executives", which necessitated that they should pick role models from among world leaders from whom they would learn some basic leadership values. The unfortunate thing in the African experience is that the new leaders picked their colonial masters or were conditioned/forced to pick their colonial oppressors as models. In the confused network, these leaders failed to be good "schoolboy" – to learn from their followers and to build team psychological safety (49). Based on the influence of their poor models and on poor personal emotional intelligence, these leaders developed cognitive biases and destroyed the team psychological safety (Bennis, 51-2). These leaders have become tyrants and continually depend on their models for military might in a bid to maintain power and control over their followers. This loyalty has brought Africa to its knees, and so literarily African nations are independent but in practice they are dependent.

The poet perceives independence as a destination towards which Africans set-out for ten years after the Second World War. Here reference is being made to the wind of change/revolution and independence that blew across Africa in the 1950^s and 60^s. Although African states got their independence from the colonial master, the poet thinks that we are still on the move towards independence's home. This idea is brought up in the poem "Until Independence Home We Arrive". The title of the poem signals the notion of movement and this is an onward process which is taking us to a definite destination – independence's home. The poem opens with a rhetorical question in which the persona desires to know whether African nations have reached the delightful home of independence. He writes:

> But tell me! Have we arrived
> As we saunter to full independence. (44)

According to the poem, the journey towards independence is still very long. Although part of the journey was covered in the last century, there is still a tedious way with "vales" and "dales" that have to be crossed. The poet is quick to note that some of the difficulties or obstacles on the way to independence have been placed by us-"some glens and hills we've even mounted ourselves". He evokes the thoughts of those who think that Africa can't succeed without help from the west. He also blames African leaders who serve or function like puppets; always dumb about the state of affairs in Africa because they feel that "word from over the salty waters (will be) sent" to them. Through the images of "puppet", "words" and "salty waters", the poet succeeds to convey in vivid terms the weakness of African leaders who rule their countries for the interest of Europe and America because they are afraid of threats "words" of deposition from western governments. Indirectly therefore the poet is advocating African leadership that will lead the continent to true independence; independence which is not based on connivance with other foreign powers to drain the continent of its resources. The poet considers the journey towards "full independence" to be a leisurely and careless walk and so he tells Africans "be not frail till that home we reach".

African nations are not yet independent because their memories are fresh with wounds of neo-colonialism. The many things to toil for include the healing of old wounds and the exploitation of new possibilities for Africa's people. One of such is to stop being mere consumers because "we weren't born to consume all our lives" (48). This message of strive towards a real Africa continues in "Still Many Things to Toil For"; from the title the poet is of the opinion that there are yet many things that Africans have to do. The poet-speaker imagines the huddles that Africans have gone through and stress is an affair that will soon give way or would be forever. This is because "ahead of us" there are still many steep and rugged rocks to climb. Africa must follow the American pattern which the poet talks about in "The American Example". Like America, Africa must fight to take off the blind of neo colonialism in order to feel freely, think freely and dream freely.

The consequences of undemocratic leadership in Africa are bad governance, bureaucracy, propaganda, deceit, hypocrisy, and wars. Ndah takes up these issues in different poems and either traces the cause, reveals its manifestation or decries its effect on the people. In "Elections Rigging Panaxia", he states that the source of Africa's numerous problems is bad governance:

> Just one Mahogany-like thorn
> In Africa's flesh resides.
> The fountain of our sundry maladies it is now.
> Bad governance this huge thorn is.
> Flawed electoral processes father this thorn.

The image of mahogany that is used to describe the thorn points to the hardness of the object. There is a double connotation in the idea of the thorn- a thorn is stiff, sharp-pointed and a mahogany is hard. This shows that the amount of pain and trouble that Africa is going through as a result of bad governance is double fold. The process of bad governance is called into being by faulty electoral systems; it is instituted and protected by bad legal frameworks.

Bad governance breeds evils such as corruption, embezzlement and wanton misuse of the financial resources of African nations. In this system of governance, the few who hold and manage power tend to engage in the misuse of the nation's resources. They are those whom the poet refers to as "a handful of robbers" when he says:

> Verily, verily unto you I say!
> Just a handful of armed robbers
> Holding high offices in high quarters, drain
> With impunity the dividends of the labour of our hands (2)

The proletariat is considered to be victims of the system of governance which allows a few to amass the nation's wealth in uncontrollable ways. The phrase "a handful of robbers" metaphorically conceptualizes and compares the number of citizens who suffer as a result of the activities of highly irresponsible individuals placed in positions of power. The poet satirises leaders who hold high positions for squandering with recklessness the resources that belong to the masses. The anger grows as he realises that these individuals parade the streets "arrogantly" and "unperturbed". There is no system of punishment for those who cripple the economy of the nation. He cries out against the misuse of the nation's funds for the buying of expensive cars while the masses are perpetually in need. He says:

> From my bowels from my marrow comes this truth on the street of
> Africa just take a look.
> Look at the myriad of limousines,
> And other automobiles,
> Peep into the residence of our armed robbers,
> Then return and tell me whether a motor park of costly cars they
> harbour in their enclosures or not.
> Adjacent such residents, you fine multiple hut-like houses of have nots
> With myriad of them held captive by pauperization

The poet's message comes from deep within his being; it is a message of truth that he feels deep in his intrinsic being. As spokesperson of the masses he feels the compulsion to speak out against such excesses. The poet tactically does not just reveal the truth but invites the reader to participate in experiencing it. By asking the reader to take a look at the street, the poet avoids the situation of abstract reporting and so involves the reader in the experience. In this way, the act and its effects are lived on the reader's mind.

The reader becomes the reporter because he/she is the one to "return and tell me whether a motor park of costly cars they harbour in their enclosure or not". While the leaders move in limousine and other expensive automobiles and live in "residents" the masses live in "hut-like houses" with deplorable conditions. The pauperization of the masses is not consequent upon the lack of resources but on the greed of those in power. This is conveyed through the use of the numerical adjective "myriad". There is the juxtaposition of the "myriad of limousine" owned by the embezzlers and "myriad of them" (have-nots) who populate the nation and live without basic means. From this, one can deduce that just as there are innumerable luxurious cars on the streets so are there innumerable beggars. Therefore if the leaders were to tamper their greed then each of the myriad limousines (wealth) will belong to the glorious place it was created to be. This however is not attainable and that is why the poet spits out more anger:

> Very bitter is the nitty-gritty that the wealth of our nations
> By few unarmed but protected robbers in high places is squandered.
> In plenty food you find but folk perish in hunger
> Folk are thirsty but everywhere water you find
> The key of our barn and tank by the spoilt is kept. (2-3)

From what the persona says, it is evident that it is the greed of the leaders that has brought ruin to postcolonial African nations. Some individuals waste the wealth. Historically, therefore, the poet's concern is on the flagrant embezzlement of state resources in Cameroon. He criticizes the fact that the Cameroonian masses live on the banks of a river but are made to wash their hands with spittle. In the midst of plenty of food and abundance of water the people live in hunger and thirst because of the greedy attitude of the leaders.

Ndah communicates the sense of abundance and depravity by drawing images from the communal wisdom of his people. Culturally speaking, the images of the "barn", the "tank" and key carry far deeper connotations than the words can express in normal usage. Usually, in the region from which the poet hails a barn is a symbol of plenty and regularized consumption so that food can be available all year round; the key is kept by the father or mother or any trustworthy child. By employing the image of the barn, the poet is suggesting that the key is in the hands of plunderers and that the real owners cannot have access to the resources. The use of the "spoils" is well calculated as it brings to mind not only the simple fact of plunder but reveals vividly the Marxist binarism and conflict between the oppressor and the oppressed, the government and citizens. The oppressor in this case is the government and is symbolised by those in "high places"; the oppressed are the citizens and in the conflict between the two, the resources become spoil which the government deprive the people of. The word "spoilt" is also used to show the degree of 'badness' or immorality of those in bungles in power. Their interest therefore is not on good governance which the poet recommends in the last stanza of the poem but on how fast and well they can plunder the "wealth of our nations" (2).

Unlike in "Win Back Our Escapees" in which the poet invites the reader to look at the streets and into the residence of the leaders to understand the wantonness in African leadership, in "Robbing Widows Mite" he confronts the leaders directly. The language is somewhat confrontational as it addresses and dares such embezzlers directly. He asks in a rather challenging manner:

> How you dare furnish your numbed bellies
> With the scarce coins of the masses?

> Before playing hanky-pankies
> With state coffers, people's coffers,
> know now the destitute souls you butcher and rob:
> (20)

The image of insensitive and insatiate arrogance of the leaders is evoked through the description of their bellies as "numbed". It is because they are insensitive to the plight of the people that they play "hanky-pankies" with the resources of the nation. The intension is therefore to call their attention to the evil that they are doing to the nation. This direct and confrontational tone continues in the second stanza as the speaker says:

> This lot for the state coffer denotes.
> How you dare, a single soul, plunders
> Thousands, millions, even billions
> For yourself and for your family alone?

The direct confrontation that characterizes these two stanzas is born out of anger over the fact that thousands of people contribute money to the nation's coffers and an individual loots all of it. The persona does not come to terms with the degree of wantonness and greed. This possibly is why to him statesmen are unscrupulous. He says:

> Unscrupulous as they are
> These so called statesmen, decision makers,
> League and throw sumptuous feasts,
> Host sumptuous summits,
> Erect castles and mansions,

> Invest in alienations,
> Stash stolen funds in alien Banks,
> Travel; at will while the masses,
> Oh! The rightful fund raisers,
> In woe and poverty stay

This is a somewhat careful enumeration of the extravagant ventures of the leaders, and this is what makes the African nation poor. The persona understands that the African masses are the ones who toil to produce wealth for the nations. This is the reason for which he laments their plight. The emotional intensity of his lament is communicated through the exclamation phrase "oh!" This is an expressive cry of pain or terror through the poet's mind over the situation of the masses or the expression of shame, derisive astonishment or disapprobation over the acts of the leaders, and the plight of the masses. This is marked by the use of action verbs at the beginning of each line of verse from line 3 to line 8 - "league" "host" "erect" "invest" and "stash". This is followed by the repetitive use of the inflectional plural marker "s" in all the nouns from line 2 to 9 - "markers", "feasts", "summits", "mansions", "Banks", "masses", "nations", and "raisers". The use of plural markers, especially in the first six words, is meant to show the excess in such acts as investing or stashing in foreign banks. This sibilant sound suggests the degree of successiveness in the activities that ruin the nation.

The wanton use of national resources is a continuous and repetitive process.

Bad leadership is manifested in the bureaucratic and inefficient structures that the government puts in place. Bureaucratic and inefficient administration has a profound effect not only on the workers but also on their families. The poet satirises this form of administration through the voice of a child who laments the plight of the father and wonders in agony whether the father will ever smile again. The poem "Will Dad Ever Smile Again" is a powerful satire spoken through the mouth of a child who juxtaposes his kindergarten days when his dad came home with smiles and goodies to the present when dad comes home from the capital with "emptiness" and "maladies". This poem is particularly interesting and contextual because it is written with a defined focus. Ndah abandons the escapist attitude expressed in others by speaking in general terms about Africa and narrows the focus to the soaring bureaucracy of his immediate Cameroon nation. The poem opens with a dialogue between two of dad's children:

> Where is dad?
> Ever in the capital?
> Doing what there?
> Ever chasing dossiers. (27)

The inquiring child has noticed that their father is almost always absent from home and so he asks the brother the whereabouts of dad only to be told that he is "ever in the capital" to follow-up his documents. The poet's diction and the whole experience in the poem are typical of what obtains in Cameroonian ministerial departments. The phrase "chasing dossiers", which suggests the process of following up files, is common usage not only around ministries in Cameroon but also among civil servants whom the poet describes as "men of diverse woes".

The speaker situates the "two huge buildings" - the Ministry of Public Service and the Ministry of Finance as the places where civil servants assemble to check whether their problems have been solved. The poet is bearing testimony to the horror of bureaucratic administrative processes in government offices in Cameroon. While the Ministry of Public Service is responsible for personnel matters involving all government employees in Cameroon and the Ministry of Finance is among other things charged with the financial situation of workers. The poet therefore locates two strategic ministries not necessarily because of their importance but because of the ordeal that civil servants go through in these ministries. The description of the ministry of finances the "money minded ministry" is intend to show the degree of corruption that goes on in it. That is why the poet says "in the ministries, small things are hardly denied" (27). The phrase "small thing" refers to the bribe that is given to facilitate the processing of peoples' files. This suggests that bribery is a common occurrence. Bribery is a consequence of a highly centralised system of government where "everything is crammed / Government from the people is far" (27). Consequently:

> "Those two ministries"...
> "Are ever crammed with men of sundry aches.
> Some come to wail for no salary,
> Some for advancements, some for arrears,
> Others are groundlessly retrenched
> Some due to untimely retirement declaration
> Some for voluntary retirement,
> Some for recruitment in the public sector,
> Some toiling to give bribes,
> Some striving to see only a particular Monsieur X.
> (28)

The anaphoric use of "Some" is meant to show that these ministries cause varied and various problems to workers. The repetition of "Some" defines the indeterminate number of people that cram these ministries. It also facilitates the categorisation of the problems civil servants are going through in the postcolonial Cameroon nation. These problems result from administrative bottle-necks and poor documentation. Files are always either "pending a signature" or they are "left" or even lost. In the horror of this confused setup, "Exhausted chasers of dossiers" with "parched throats" sit disorderly under trees and "their sundry worries they chat about the pain" (29).

There is a sense of comic tragedy because Dad tells this story of the woe in the ministry as fun to calm "flaring tempers". However, the experience has had a very negative effect on Dad in the sense that he is frustrated to the extent that he no longer smiles and so the poem ends with the rhetorical question that is its title: "will dad ever smile again?" Bad leadership characterised by bureaucratic structures, corruption and poor documentation has a negative effect on the lives of the citizens.

In the opinion of Emmanuel A. Anyambod[viii], the problem of immigration that postcolonial nations are facing and which Ndah handles meticulously can be blamed on bad leadership. He analyses the motives to migrate in terms of "incentives attracting people away, known as pull factors, (and) circumstances encouraging a person to leave, known as push factors" (4). To Anyambod, Africa's passwords are poverty, misery, corruption, war and drought yet Africa is "a wonderful landscape endowed with the abundance of riches…" Thus, he avers: "If the resources in Africa are well used by African leaders, the …push factor can easily be addressed, life made better for all Africans, hence the needless movement for the search of jobs abroad" (5). Anyambod therefore blames the great movement out of Africa on the inability of African leaders to properly harness the resources for the good of the nations. Even the senseless wars which devastate the continent are a consequence of bad leadership policies. The poet describes leaders as "war provokers" or "Elephant at a helm" who constantly engage in conflicts that bring untold suffering on the masses. The criticism of the present state of African leadership is a call for change; a call for a new order or system of leadership that rules for the good of the masses and the nation. The kind of society that he advocates is

> "one marked by moral decency, and rid of economic and political abuse, a society where there is social justice and fairness in the distribution of the wealth of the nation and not one in which this sharing is skewed in favour of the rich and the powerful, a society devoid of electoral chicanery, gerrymander, corruption and the violation of the human rights of defenceless citizens. (Ambanasom, 2)

This is the mission of the poet - to conscientize society; to warn leaders about the possible dangers of poor/bad leadership and to awaken the people to the evil of political authority as well as give them hope of a better life, especially if they stand against such corrupt leadership systems. Nyah confronts the leadership of postcolonial Cameroon and African in daring ways – appealing to their sense of conscience at some points and challenging their humanness in others. The poet, like most Anglophone Cameroon and postcolonial African poets, rightly thinks that the predicament of the postcolonial Cameroon nations results from the wanton exploitation of national resources for personal profit.

CHAPTER FIVE
REVOLUTIONARY TENDENCIES IN ALOBWED'EPIE'S *CRYING IN HICCOUGHS*

The revolutionary currents in Alobwed'Epie's poetry are the direct product of his society. The environment in which the poet finds himself and the social and political realities play upon the imagination of the poet and the result is such a soulful cry for a people and a nation caught in the grip of a power elite that has rendered life meaningless. Leon Trotsky in "The Social Roots and the Social Function of Literature" quotes Shklovsky argument on the environment and how it influences the theme of literature. Shklovsky is quoted to have said: "If the environment and the relations of production influenced art, then would not the themes of art be tied to the places which would correspond to these relations? But themes are homeless" (Troysky). Trotsky however warns that "To say that man's environment, including the artist's, that is, the conditions of his education and life, find expression in his art also, does not mean to say that such expression has a precise geographic, ethnographic and statistical character" (Trotsky). Poetry is the transformation of the ethnographic and statistical experiences of the poet's own life into phantasmagorias by means of turning into the self under the power of a new stimulus. Alobwed'Epie therefore builds from the innate part of his being, the conviction that only revolutionary action can restore the lost glory of the postcolonial Cameroon nation or provide avenues for the construction of new vision for the nation.

In "My Little Song", Alobwed'Epie captures the spirit and essence of poetry in a postcolonial context where people are either deaf or dumb or blind to the power of revolution that poetry and writing in general can provide. The function of poetry as a tool of societal conscientization is evoked in such a powerful way that the reader has little options left than to join the poet and "sing, sing, sing aloud" (1). The role of the poet as a singer is also forcefully conveyed and is done with a degree of melodiousness that at once reveals that the poet is a real singer. The use of phone aesthetics or music evoking devices is central to the understanding of how the poet becomes a singer in other to infiltrate the senses of the reader and awaken them from their deafness, dumbness and blindness. The alliteration conveyed in the recurrence of the sibilant /s/ sound in "So, my little song I'll sing to myself" and "And we'll sing and sing and sing aloud" (1) suggests a sensational attachment to the songs, and a sensitive appeal to the decayed senses of the reader.

The poet wants to touch the emotional core of the audience and bring them to the point of crescendo where they will reason like him and join in the singing. There is also the technique of repetition in the poem which closely aligns it to music and the idea of appealing to the emotional sensibility of the deceased audience.

Alobwed'Epie's intension, as mentioned in this poem, is to fight the devil that has taken hold of his people in the postcolonial Cameroon nation. This first poem in the collection establishes the revolutionary tone that most of the poems express. Poetry is a powerful tool in the hand of a great craftsman: like philosophy it breaks the spell of ignorance that leadership has imposed on the people; like prayer it exorcises the mind and strengthens it against all forms of lethargy, and like music it stirs the emotions of those that read and lifts them up from the doldrums of fear and insecurity into which they have been immersed. The poet therefore thinks that poetry is a veritable instrument with which he can cast away hex or break the concentric circles of terror, horror and barrenness that leadership has built around the people. Accordingly, therefore the decayed state of the people is not a natural phenomenon; it is a condition created by the power elite intended to keep the people perpetually under the control of the leader. As a seer and conscience of the society, the poet feels the urgent need to shake the people out of this spell.

The function and meaning of poetry is measured in purely Marxist terms. This is another signal of the strong revolutionary undercurrent of Alobwed'Epie's poetry. The song can only have meaning or be considered useful if it calls the people to action against a system that has blinded, deafened and muted them. When the audience hears him and talks to him or joins him in pulling the leaders down from the "top of the ladder.../ Then, shall my little song have meaning" (1). Alobwed'Epie is trying to prove to the masses that as a poet his job is to think only of them, live only for them and love them 'terribly' even more than he loves himself.

In order for the audience to hear him and join in revolutionary action, he needs to speak to them in a language that they understand. He needs to take the position of a prophet speaking not in sublime extra-terrestrial language but in the language of the people. He needs to consider himself a man talking to other men, admonishing them to take a course which by his divine poetic wits will bring salvation to the nation and its people. In defining his choice of language for poetry, Alobwed'Epie employs striking juxtaposition to bring out the necessity for the poet to speak to the people in the language they understand in "My Song in Silver" wherein the poet-speaker says:

> I do not cloak my song in gold
> But in silver bright for the lowly
> For silver appeals to the masses
> And gold to the 'greedy' few. (1)

Alobwed'Epie in these lines seeks justification for the way he has chosen to use his poetic license. He writes in this poem and others (even in his novels) with the consciousness of a grammarian targeting a particular audience with a particular message and tries as much as possible not to corrupt the register or tilt the meaning gradient between him and his audience. The language of poetry especially poetry with a political agenda that speaks to the soul of the masses continue to be a problematic issue to address. All poets claim to be speaking to the masses somewhere at some point in time. The question then is: can the language of steel and complicated syntactic jigsaw of Bate Besong or can the complex phraseology, puzzling adjectivised nouns and incongruous imagistic pattern of Wirndzerem G. Barfee[ix] speak to the masses as much the same way as the measured, symbolic but simplistic hymnal verses of Ernest Veyu[x] or Alobwed'Epie's calculated, direct and imagistic verses. While the debate may be rife with philosophy or common logic, the position Alobwed'Epie states it clearly – to speak to the people use language that is accessible to them. In his logic therefore, distant references to ancient gods of Greece and Athens or severe distortion of language should be used in poetry that is written for the "'greedy' few" – most probably referring to those with the gift of scholarly and critical aptitude, those positively greedy for knowledge.

Alobwed'Epie's philosophy of the relationship between the ruling elite and the masses is closely associated to the philosophical ideology of John Locke as described in the Social Contract as the poet insistently talks about the need for the masses to exercise their right and revolt against the ruling class for failing to fulfil their part of the contract. "Bang Your Doors" is symbolic of an open call for the masses to revolt against those who come to them during political elections to tell lies or make false promises. The poet admonishes the people to stop dancing to welcome these "foul-mouthed" liars who have been sent to come and convince them with a pack of lies:

> Stop dancing, you bearers of the bier,
> They have wrecked the land, don't you see?
> If you don't, your shrivelled jaw bones tell,
> Bang your doors, Midas is amok. (34)

The poet is conscious of the plight of the masses even when they are not. This is what makes him a poet and a distinct individual in the society with the power of vision. In an exploitative society like the one in which the poet finds himself, it is his responsibility to defy the forces that work continuously to destroy the freedom of the people. He awakens the people to the realities of their conditions; noting that even if they cannot see that the very people they are dancing for are the ones who have ruined the nation, then their shrunken jaws should be evidence of their condition. It is this responsibility that makes the poet an outcast especially to those whose source of power depends on the exploitation of the common man. Kenneth Rexroth in "The Function of Poetry and the Place of the Poet in Society" points to the outcast status of the poet when he, talking to a community of poets at a congress says:

> Our most significant poets, whatever limited prestige and reputations they may enjoy, are nonetheless outcasts from this society. We may not all of us be extraordinarily distinguished or considered tremendously significant in the world of letters, but insofar as we are poets, we are enemies of this present society.

The present society in the context of Cameroon is the powerful, exploitative and fear instilling governing class that the poet engages in a struggle to liberate the people from their manipulative and abusive tendencies. The poet is an outcast because he is a crusader for the masses; he is a visionary of truth.

The title of the poem "Bang Your Doors" which is repeated in the poem is a symbol of rejection and revolution. The people are advised to reject these "mailed Ambassadors" who have come to preach a message which is not true. The people should bang their doors because if they listen to the emissaries of the regime and do not yield to it, other means would be used to win them over such as cash or mysticism: "Midas is amok and full of intrigues, / He has the cash and the wand, / Where one fails the other will succeed, / Your best bed, bang your doors" (34). The tone of the poem is that of both supplication and confrontation. The poet beseeches his people to rebel against the political "Ambassadors" that have come to "Deceive the Masses". Yet at the same time he confronts the politicians as evident in the words he uses to describe them: "Callous Plunderer", "mailed Ambassadors lying", "saponaceous shame-proof faces", "hackers", "Midas is amok" and "full of intrigues". The word choice shows proof of the poet's anger and antagonism against such politicians. To show the contrast between the politician and the masses that they exploit, the poet repeats the image of jaws in stanza one and stanza three. In the first instance, the jaws of the politicians are described as "balloon jaws" and then latter those of the masses are described as "shrivelled jaws". The jaw is a measuring standard for healthy living – while the politicians who loot the wealth of the nation have healthy puffy jaws, the masses they have come to deceive have sunken jaws, which is evidence of their horrifying condition.

The most daring appeal for revolutionary action in the poetry of Alobwed'Epie can be read in "Our Byzantium Day" in which the poet comes out clearly and loudly to call for a revolution because the youths are not just living a terrible lie but are incessantly being reformulated into other lies. The speaker in "Our Byzantium Day" is a middle age man who has come to the sudden realization that he and his generation have been living a lie for all their years and so he calls on his peers to join him in revolutionary action even though conscious that it will not be an easy undertaking. They spent their childhood years celebrating a feast which was meant to nurse romantic nationalist dreams in their minds about the possibilities of taking command someday. Now that they are already adults, possibly ready and poised to take control of the nation's destiny, they realize that all that they had been told and made to do and believe are lies because even those dads whom they marched to hail are bent on remaining in power. The only option that seems to present itself is revolution against the system. The last four of the nine stanzas of the poem encapsulates the philosophy of revolt and goes thus:

> We wriggle in pain and cause alarm,
> Yet, on deaf ears that surely falls,
> When patience loses its charm of hope,
> The only option, defy the rule.
>
> We once did, and six lay dead,
> Our goody dads slew their heirs,
> There's a goblin in each black head
> Dread it not, and you will be dead.

> You'll be dead but be not scared,
> In whatever way, you are dead,
> Die fighting, never surrendering
> Our only option, fight it on.
>
> There's glory dying on the field,
> It's a shame shying away,
> Move forward, never backward,
> Mandela did, and won our wills. (33)

The instigation of revolutionary action is so clear, so strong and so direct that it makes commentary almost useless because the poet does not hide his sentiments in any cryptic symbols or images. Through the juxtaposition of the "Byzantium day" of his childhood and the harsh realities of his adulthood the speaker establishes a strong rationale for revolutionary action. The pleasant or romanticized vision of the speaker and his generation can be better understood if the title of the poem is placed in the context of W.B Yeats' vision of Byzantium as a world of phantasmagoric beauty. Byzantium days therefore refer to the dreamy beauty they were made to have about their nation and their future. They were given false images of the Cameroon nation and made to belief that in due time they will take over and be the leaders of the nation. The first five stanzas follow each other and develop from the innocence to the moment of complaint when the speaker fully understands the implications of what they did and the complications of belonging to a nation where young people are imbued with lies about a national spirit of devotion and patriotism. In castigating the falsehood that is taught to children on national days, Alobwed'Epie re-echoes Oscar C. Labang's profound cry in the poem "My Country Took A Wrong Turn" that:

>My country is dying of thirst in the heart of a desert
>Me and my generation discovered we had been told a lie
>We had been made to sing songs with little meaning
>Songs we sang with vim and vigour
>Trusting in the nation we were taught to serve
>
>The lyrics ring still in my brain
>*I was born a Cameroonian*
>*I shall live a Cameroonian*
>*I shall die a Cameroonian*
>*I am proud to be a Cameroonian*
>
>We sang with joy and love
>We sang with hope and aspirations
>We sang with pride and self-importance
>We sang for our fatherland
>But now where is the fatherland? Where is it?
>
>We realized we had been shown another path
>And the owners of the country were on another.
>Now our conscience ask us questions we can't answer
>And those whose faltering lips manage to speak

Throw curses on whoever taught them the songs (8-9)

Both poets lament a process that has become almost a custom in which young Cameroonians are taught songs of patriotism and national pride but when they grow to a certain age they come to the realization that all were smokescreens behind which the nation was being sapped to destruction. Alobwed'Epie and Labang are therefore of the opinion that the attitude towards the values of nationalism should change. They are advocating a revolt by young Cameroonians against a status-quo that has kept them permanently at a loss. The generational disparity between the two poets and the fact that they bemoan the same issue points to the fact that this is a process that has been going on for a very long time, and the poets think that it is time for change.

In a bid to capture the attention of the reader and to infuse his message of revolution in them, Alobwed'Epie exploits the ignorance and innocence of an African child to appeal for the need for revolution in the poem "The Weeping African Child". The weeping child in this poem is a strong agent of revolt who does not call for activist revolutionary action as is the case in other poems but subtly tells the people and the leaders some profound truths that are more radical than action. By making the child an "African child", the poet gives the child's message a universal African perspective, suggesting that the experience that the child conveys is common to many, if not all, African children.

The simplicity of the language and the repetitive pattern of the first line are symptoms of a child-like expression pattern. Through the simple and straight forward language of the child, the poet digs into some of the core values of leadership that have been clearly violated by African leaders. The reckless embezzlement of public funds and the reckless looting of national resources is one of the major leadership problems that the child talks about to his people. The child is conscious of the fact that the leaders are thieves who have paid themselves already by looting the coffers of the nation. He says:

> We owe our leaders nothing
> They've paid themselves in kind
> In looting our gold and silver
> Leaving us to die in want. (12)

The child is a victim of the politician's greed because he exists in a context where leadership does not care about the plight of children. They have been blinded by greed and so it becomes increasingly difficult for them to be conscientious. The child knows that his nation is endowed with resources that can be used to better his life and that of other children. That is why he talks about the "silver" and "gold" with which the leaders have paid themselves. The juxtaposition of "paid" and loot is central to the understanding of the concept of embezzlement in African nations. This can be seen in the fact that unlike in other nations where the salary of the leaders are known publicly and even questioned in some cases, the salaries of most African leaders are unknown to anybody. In this way, the leader can comfortably loot all the country's wealth in the guise of a salary. The child in this poem knows the realities of the society, and equally knows that he and others are the victims as he goes back to the effect of the actions of the leaders on their lives:

> We owe our leaders nothing
> Though we must sing their praises
> We know the cow is milked to death
> And our lives are brought to nought. (12)

Here again, the child is trying to conscientize his people about the ills of the leaders and why they do not owe the leaders anything. The image of gold and silver in the first stanza of the poem gives way to a more comprehensive and culturally binding image – that of a cow that is being milked. The cow is suggestive of the wealth of the nation that the leaders are exploiting for their personal benefit. Even more intriguing, the cow has a certain emotional functionality especially when it is associated to the child speaking in the poem. When the leaders loot the gold and silver, the consequence on the child and others is that they are left wanting. But when the leaders milk the cow, it means even the basic necessities of childhood like milk is denied the children. This is the peak of exploitation, where leaders deprive the people of even the very basic things needed for daily existence. When children are deprived of milk then the only possible thing left is that their "lives are brought to nought" (12). Like the cow that is milked to death, the child who depends on the cow for milk can at best slowly and gradually die. Even as the child watches their lives waste to nothingness, he is ironically conscious of yet another tribute that they must pay to the leaders – "we must sing their praises" (12).

The central motif in the poem is the child's ability to diagnose the ills of his society and to call the people to revolutionary action. Through the refrain the child continually instils in the mind of the reader and the African people the fact that leadership is demanding recompense that the people do not owe them because of the crimes they have committed against the people. By repeating the line "We owe our leaders nothing", the child not only creates emphasis and shows simplistic repetition but also sustains the idea of refusal to pay the leaders throughout the poem. He continually pokes the issue because he thinks that it is central. This is clear evidence of a rebellious African child calling others to rebel against the leadership by refusing to pay them because the leaders have not done anything that deserves pay. They have been at the centre of the destruction of the continent, and the injuring and killing of their parents through "senseless and dirty wars". The child therefore does not see any reason to compensate the leaders. The last stanza of the poem touches the core of revolution and creates the necessity for rebellion:

> We owe our leaders nothing
> They build the dungeon larger
> And there they cram and torture
> All who dare raise alarm (13)

The child stands the chance of being tortured in one of such dungeons because of the consciousness that he instils in his people through this poem. The idea of torture of political activists parallels the situation of Creature in John Nkemngong Nkengasong's play *Black Caps and Red Feather* wherein a leader with similar tendencies as the one castigated by the child, incarcerates Creature because he dares to tell the clan the truth about the miserable conditions of life and about the death of some national heroes. In this play, Nkengasong decries the exploitation of the clan by Traourou and his men, and calls the people of the clan to revolutionary action with the aim of saving it from the tyranny and greed of the leadership. Like Creature who is tortured in the prison and rendered half psychotic, it is evident from the last remarks of the child that African nations are ruled by tyrants who do not spare the opportunity of arresting and imprisoning whoever seeks to call the people to consciousness. The dungeon refers to the prisons that are being erected for the incarceration of political activists. As one who has "raise(d) alarm" about the need to rebel and refuse to pay the leaders for various reasons, the child is a potential occupant of the dungeon. The child and Creatures are agents of revolutionary action; they are visionaries of truth and they stand against the forces of exploitation, fear, insecurity and tyranny that continually beset African nations.

The central motif in the poem is the weeping child's ability to diagnose the ills of his society and to call the people to revolutionary action. A similar motif recurs in "The Crying Street Man" in which the common man bemoans his plight in a nation where "patrons" dictate the pace of his life according to their whims and caprices. Like the child, the man is in a state of psychological pain and frustration; this is possibly the reason for which he is crying. Through the pain of the man, Alobwed'Epie successfully identifies and condemns some of the excesses of postcolonial leadership.

The recurrent image of emotional stress is expressed in "crying" and "weeping" as suggested in the title of the collection *Crying in Hiccough*. Alobwed'Epie continually evokes the image to show that the people for whom he speaks are going through an emotional state that is not pleasant. V. Patel defines crying as "a complex secretomotor phenomenon characterized by the shedding of tears from the lacrimal apparatus, without any irritation of the ocular structures". The crying of the author and that of the personae in the poems can be explained from the temporary perspective as well as from the private-public perspective.

The temporal perspective in the opinion of Jack Katz in *How Emotions Work* shows that sorrowful crying is due to looking to the past with regret or to the future with dread (182). The weeping of the African child and the crying of the man on the street results partly from the fact that they have examined their fate and that of their nation and found that the course taken by leadership is that which will lead the country to doom and destruction. The temporary perspective is also crying that results from the loss of someone and regretting not spending more time with them or being nervous about an upcoming event (Jack Katz, 182). The child's view of the past is full of regret because it is characterized by greed, exploitation, wars and torture. His view of the present and the future is typified by trauma and trepidation because he is conscious of the fact that he is compelled to be a sycophant of the leadership though he is even more conscious of the milking of the cow, the maiming and killing of elders in wars and the building of prisons to torture those who oppose such wanton destruction of the countries' resources. Similarly, the Street Man's cry is an expression of nervousness about upcoming events which he outlines from the beginning to the end of the poem. His existence is conditioned by what the "patrons" do or do not do and this creates in the man intense emotions that cause him to cry. Both the child and the man are, to use Alan Paton's words, crying for the beloved country hijacked by bad leaders.

The public-private perspective defines crying for joy or sorrowful crying as two ways to imply details about the self as known privately or one's public identity (Jack Katz, 182). Crying resulting from a loss is an appeal to the outside world for help with coping with internal sufferings. The internal tension in the child in "The Weeping African Child" is what has caused the child to reach out to others. The poem then becomes a public appeal to other children to consider what the condition in which the leaders have led their nation. This public appeal is an effort to cope with "internal suffering" (Jack Katz, 182). The emotive passion of crying from a private-public perspective takes a more intense form in "The Cry of the Street Man" because the poem is an ejaculation of what is going on in his consciousness as conveyed in the first line refrain "Now I know" (13). The diction of this simple line of verse is dense with meaning. The word "now" is both an indication of time and the state of mind of the speaker; it is an indication of 'the present time' as well as a pointer to the fact that the speaker is annoyed about something. From these perspectives, the poem becomes an expression of what the speaker is going through at the moment when he is speaking. It is also indicative of the speaker's annoyance at the fact that the "patrons" eat their share and his then frowns when they realize that he knows what they have done. The speaker is annoyed over the fact that the leaders use the "baton" to silence him and force him to bed when they want to dance. The phrase "Now" takes an even more functional literary relevance when it is "used to get somebody's attention before changing the subject or asking them to do something" (Oxford Advanced). The recurrence of this phrase as the first line of every stanza is important because each stanza takes up a new line of thought or reveals a new experience that the speaker is going through in the hands of the "patrons". The speaker therefore seeks to grab the readers' attention at each stage before telling them what the patrons are doing or will do and how it will affect him. His crying therefore continually holds the reader's thoughtfulness because of the desire to know what the speaker knows.

The cry in *Crying in Hiccoughs* also has greater meaning in the context of the private-public perspective especially in relation to the idea of expressing the individual's public identity. The crying in the title of the collection is that of the author, crying in different ways, with different emotional intensity and at different times because of the anger and angst that he harbours. Poetry thus becomes a soulful cry from the innate being of the poet as he seeks to speak to his people about the ills of insensitive leadership and to speak to leadership about the consequences of their action on the citizenry. The poet's cry is so penetrating that even amidst hiccoughs he cannot stop crying; he has to cry in hiccoughs because of the continuous decay that is taking over the nation and the African continent as a whole. His tears are thus expressed in the last stanza of "These Tears", one of the poems that carry the central image of crying, in a more imagistic pattern:

> These tears, long and heavy,
> With petals folded my morn is past
> With clipped lips I watch in awe,
> My assigned stone-laden pit (14)

The image of tears "Furrowing my spiked cheeks" or "shawling the glow in my star" is central in this poem and serves again as a recurrent linguistic item which conveys a deep emotional and psychological stress. Like "Weeping African Child" and "Cry of the Street Man", "These Tears" depend heavily on the refrain of the first line to evoke emotions of tears about the state of the speaker in the mind of the reader. The sixteen line poem with relative short verses repeat the line "These tears, long and heavy" at the beginning of each stanza before communicating every new experience that the speaker has. The crying or tears of the poet like those of the personae in the poem are psychic tears

– "produced by the lacriminal system and are the tears expelled during emotional states" (Lutz, *Crying*, 68).

In "Depleted Harvest" there is an ambitious use of images all of which speak to the chaos of exploitation, the barbarism of postcolonial leadership, the collapse of values and institution and the trauma of living in such a nation. In this short four stanza poem of seventeen lines, Alobwed'Epie shows seasoned mastery of a blend of images with daring revolutionary undercurrents and different semantic twists. Underneath these images, Alobwed'Epie slides a subtle call for revolution as he stands back and with refined poetic sensibility re-examines the fate of the Cameroon nation in the light of the dream of his forebears. The poem is one those deep emotional cries in hiccoughs about the need for something to be done before the entire nation drowns in the chaos of postcolonial leadership. The first stanza reveals the degree of depletion of resources that is going on in the images of "harvest" that has dwindled, the "empty" pan of the beggar, the dire "want" in a land where there once was plenty and the sickening "cry" where milk was flowing. The second stanza uses images of calamity and collapse in grinding succession:

> Donkey years of chaos,
> Years of calamity,
> Our lakes explode in anger,
> Our markets pick fire at will,
> And schools collapse while standing. (21)

There is successive calamity and the lakes, the markets and the schools capture this chaos in very pictorial details. The onomatopoeia in the explosion of the lake as well as the visual sensation of fire in the market and pictographic collapse of school building create in the mind of the reader an overwhelming sense of anarchy, destruction and mayhem. This dark picture of collapse is made even worse by the dense sense of ominous forebodings conveyed in the next stanza:

> The owl hoots in mournful tones,
> The sky is cast in dark ridges,
> There's red rain at the horizon
> And mother quake in fear. (21)

The images in this excerpt are pregnant with gloom, sorrow and despair. Cosmic forces like the owl, the sky and rain are reacting to the panorama of anarchy that has engulfed life in the poet's nation. The "mournful tones" of the owl - a sign of bad omen; the "dark ridges" of the sky – a symbol of depressing emotions and bad feeling; the "red rain" – a symbol of destruction and danger; and the seism of fear has taken hold of the mothers who carry with them an impenetrable feeling of ill fate. To the poet, this can be averted because it did not constitute part of the dream of the founding fathers. Consequently, he sends a call to revolution in the last stanza:

> Let's do something to save them,
> This wasn't the dream of our forebears,
> Tell petit Jean, the Moses,

That the Red Sea is now red" (21)

This is a universal call for revolution directed especially to those who know or can imagine the dream of the founding fathers of the nation. The poet-speaker is part of the revolutionary action because he talks about "Let's". There is the urgent need to "save them" – the beggars, those in want, those crying even the years of chaos and years of calamity, the lakes, the markets and the school all need to be saved and restored to the initial dream. The last two lines of the poem express a strong revolutionary opinion. The biblical reference to Moses and the Red Sea are forces of revolution that are far stronger than the ordinary images would reveal. In the context of Cameroon, these images suggest a complete movement away from the system in place and so at once suggest the secession of Anglophone Cameroon from La Republique as the alternative for a happy existence. Within this praxis, the meaning of other images shifts and become clearer. For example, the lakes exploding in anger become an allusion to the Lake Nyos disaster that occurred in 1986, and the school collapsing refers to the collapse of the Anglophone system of education under the French system.

Revolutionary tendencies in the poetry of Alobwed'Epie take various forms from images that implicitly suggest revolution to a direct call for action against a system of government that has lost touch with the realities that its people are living. The poet uses the metaphor of crying to point to the degree of psychological trauma and emotional breakdown that different facets of the nation are experiencing. To him therefore, it is only through the open overthrow of the present system that people can experience order and a meaningful existence, and that the nation can be restored to the original dream of the forefathers.

CHAPTER SIX
BETRAYED BOND OF BROTHERHOOD: THE CRISES OF NATIONHOOD IN DZEKASHU MACVIBAN'S *SCIONS OF THE MALCONTENT*

The relationship between the two Cameroons has been a life wire for creativity for a very long time. This relationship which has been dramatized by playwrights like Epie Ngome in *What God Has Put Asunder* and narrated by novelist like John Nkemngong Nkengasong in *Across the Mongolo*, continue to be a wellspring of creative thought for young Cameroonian poets like Dzekashu MacViban. This chapter examines MacViban's vision of the problematic of nationhood between Southern Cameroon and French Cameroon. By evoking this issue in poetry, MacViban, like most Anglophone Cameroon poets, does what Nantang Jua and Piet Konings refer to as putting Anglophone nationalism on the public space when they argue that "the entry of Anglophone nationalism into public space during political liberalisation in the 1990s has posed a severe threat to the post-colonial nation-building project" (610). These two scholars note that History holds it that these two nations, which at some point were under different colonial influences from France and Britain as a result of the defeat of Germany after the First World War, opted to become one independent nation. Michael Ndobegang in "The Anglophone-Francophone Divide in Cameroon" notes that:

> Cameroon came to independence comprising people who had lived under French rule (Francophones) and those who had lived under British rule (Anglophones). There were constitutional and legal safeguards which provided protection for the two components that made up the new nation. But the much hidden, even if latent, reality in Cameroon is about a disconnected nation, a disconnection that is linked to its very bilingual nature. (1)

The very basis of this union has been questioned by writers who think that the terms of the union have been violated and one part – Anglophone Cameroon – is being marginalized. Analysing the language evolution of Cameroon from a diachronic and synchronic perspective, Augustine Simo Bobda states that "Faced with what they see as accumulated injustice perpetrated against their language, themselves and their culture, Anglophones have, after a quarter of a century of co-existence with their Francophone countrymen, started to react in all kinds of ways" ("Varying Statuses"). He shows the various ways through which these reactions are manifested, and on the artistic reaction he makes sketchy but interesting and worthwhile commentary on how some Anglophone Cameroon writers have taken up the course of Anglophone minority in their works. In line with this, it is thus understandable why a dominant theme in Anglophone Cameroon literature is the second class position of Anglophone cultures, identity and values in the dominant and domineering French (Francophone) system.

The betrayal of the bond of nationhood refers to what has been described in political terms as "a breach of trust on the part of the dominant and domineering Francophone leadership and from a lack of openness in matters of public interest" (*The Buea Declaration*). By taking up a burning issue like the abrogation of the terms of nationhood and the marginalization of Anglophones in Cameroon, the poet shares in the "apprehensions on the part of Anglophones because of what has been termed "the intolerant and hypocritical attitude of our francophone brothers..." (Ndobegang, 3). It is this intolerance and hypocrisy that resulted in the marginalization of Anglophones and what is referred to as the Anglophone problem. According to Victor Julius Ngoh the Anglophone problem is "broadly speaking, the non-participation of Anglophones, on an equal basis with Francophone, in the political, economic, social and cultural life of the nation" (Ngoh, 214). John Nkemngong Nkengasong opines that:

> The problem is defined in terms of the marginalization, assimilation, dictatorship and fake

democratic practices which have hindered Anglophone Cameroonians from having control over themselves and their destiny since British Southern Cameroons joined the French République du Cameroun in 1961 to constitute a nation. ("Interrogating the Union", 51)

This exclusion of Anglophones from the life of the nation is thus a controversial but almost always current issue in Anglophone Cameroon writing. In the novel genre John Nkemngong Nkengasong has explored this issue in *Across the Mongolo* while in drama Bole Butake examines the problematic of the relationship in *Family Saga;* Bate Besong dramatizes the fate of Anglophones who live the life of second-class citizens in Ednuoay City which is an artistic reversal of the name of the capital of "La République du Cameroun". He shows how the demand for freedom and recognition is rejected and trivialized by the Francophone regime under Aadingingin. In poetry, John Nkemngong Nkengasongs in *Letters to Marion,* Bate Besong in *The Grain of Bobe Ngom* Jua, John Ngongkum Ngong in *Walls of Agony* and *Chants of a Lunatic*, Nol Alembong in *Forest Echoes,* Mathew Takwi in *People Be Not Fooled* and *On Their Knees,* Wirndzerem G. Barfee in *Bird of the Oracular Verb* and a host of other poets have probed into the issues that beset the nation and threaten the unity. As Nkengasong notes "Analysis of Anglophone poetry, and of the poets' reaction to the legacy of colonialism, supports the argument that Anglophone Cameroon poetry articulates a network of experiences and visions to offer a severe critique of the irreconcilable union" (51).

This chapter seeks to continue the discourse on how Anglophone Cameroon poetry and poets are concerned with the vocalization of the dynamics of the problematic relationship by analysing selected poems from Dzekashu MacViban's *Scions of the Malcontent*. The focus on the poetry of Dzekashu is important because it shows that the question of Anglophone identity and the relationship with Francophones is still a current and burning issue in Anglophone Cameroon poetry. Nkengasong's analysis of the issue pays attention to the poetry of two Second Generation Anglophone Cameroonian poets; this chapter takes the discourse further by analysing the same concern in the poetry of a young Third Generation poet with the aim of showing that identity, belonging and betrayal are topical issues and that the young poet is committed to the course of his people in a manner similar to that of his poetic forebears. His role as a visionary diagnosing the political and social fabric of his society gains more currency and importance.

The poet has often been regarded as the spokesperson of the people, as one who bears the message of a force stronger than him and who must perform this function even against his own will. The poet has been thought of to have a higher ability to manipulate words and language in order to name, to order, to create experience and this gives the poet deep and fundamental social/moral responsibility and authority not possessed in the same degree by ordinary people. The overwhelming presence of the poetic message and the poet's inability to resist it is communicated in MacViban's "Genesis I". The poet is apparently burdened by a message that he is obliged to speak out or suffocate. The poet is conditioned to yield to the "rhythm of known voices". These voices haunt him and "suffocate (his) thought" (MacViban 9). He is obliged therefore by his calling as a poet to recreate the existential condition of his people in which case he laments the failure of the brotherhood between French and English Cameroons and in some instances show how Anglophones fight back Francophone marginalization.

The origin of the relationship or union of the two nations is perceived to have been doomed to failure from the very beginning. MacViban uses the image of a dark cave similar to that of Plato in the allegory of the cave to show the evil and ignorance that characterized attempts at uniting two peoples with separate and contrasting cultures and value systems. He writes:

> ... Deep within the darkness of
> The cave lies a punctured genesis.

> With two voices piercing each other
> I watched the changing scenes (9)

The dark cave is a central metaphor in understanding the punctured nature of the genesis of the relation - reunification. Darkness symbolizes on one hand the shadowy nature of the deals that brought about the union. It, on the other hand, suggests the ignorance that characterized the entire process of creating a union between an independent state French Cameroon and another state – British Southern Cameroons - seeking independence from Britain. The consequence of creating a union in such darkness is the constant rivalry which the poet refers to as "piercing each other". The constant conflict in values between the peoples of the two Cameroons and the various militarized means of subduing the people into a vision of one and inseparable nation form the "changing scenes" (9) which the poet talks about.

In a union that is founded on an erroneous vision, or in which there is constant infighting as revealed in "Genesis I", the outcome is bitterness, and frustration as each part takes its own course like the petals that fall in "Harvest of Thorns" (11). The image of thorns, used to reinforce the betrayal, frustration and bitterness of the Anglophone in the brotherhood can be found in the poem "Existence". It is a four stanza poem in which MacViban shows the existential struggle of the Anglophone as they live through "the endless night" in La Republique. The brotherhood is betrayed because the brother's embrace has ill intents as he tries to dominate and marginalize the other. The poet writes: "Brother, your embrace is full of thorns / Which try to asphyxiate our aged-old exuberance" (13). The image of thorns and the term "asphyxiating" communicate in very strong ways the degree of evil or ill intent that the brother has, and show the level to which Francophones will go to dominate Anglophones in the union. As symbolism "thorns" can yield meaning depending on the perspective from which it is read. For the brother who's embrace is full of thorns, the thorns symbolize a protective layer which is used to keep Anglophones away. It is used to create a distance or show lack of contact between the two possibly because the brother being addressed does not want to accommodate the friendship or brotherly warmth of the other. To the speaker, thorns represent a form of marginalization, torture, intimidation; a form of separation and rejection from the brother. He therefore feels betrayed. The relationship between the two brothers in this poem is reminiscent of Kamala and Kamalo in Bole Butake's *Family Saga*; a play in which Butake stages the complex and exploitative nature of the relationship between French and English Cameroons. In the context of both texts, Kamalo is the brother who is wearing thorns as a way of keeping away or differentiating himself from his brother Kamala.

Like most minority peoples or groups, the existential condition of the Anglophones is typified by struggle and fighting back the forces that work to subjugate them or define their existence in ways that are not favourable. This struggle for space in a setting where one is not recognized or is named and framed is captured in the first stanza of "Existence" where the speaker says:

> We fought back, with light, the endless night
> You imposed on our existence
> As the day had the day, never to return
> It seemed –
> Had it all ended there
> In that primeval darkness of genesis?
> You tailed us – through time and space alas! – (13)

The poet introduces a set of new images as he endeavours to communicate the innate feeling of a betrayed brother who has to fight against an existence that is fixed and imposed on him. The images of "light" and "night" are cardinal in the way they reveal the most intensive implications of the poet's world. These images are subtle yet the way they express meaning in the poet's context gives them new forms of poetic effervescence. The "we" of the first line and the "you" of the second are exclusive categories that must continually battle against each other in the struggle for a meaningful existence. They give greater significance to the images of "light" and "night" in which sense the images can both submerge the other depending on the magnitude. The "we" refers to the poet and his own part of the nation – Anglophone Cameroon, while the "you" refers to the Francophones. Apart from symbolizing the Anglophone/Francophone struggle for existential space, these terms are concepts that convey profound layers of subjugation and marginalization. The "light" represents all the various means through which Anglophones struggle to be recognized or to appropriate a voice in Cameroon; the "night" on its part represents the various methods used by Francophones to deny the Anglophone his right to equal citizenship in the nation.

The perception of the union of the Cameroons as a marriage doomed to fail or that has already collapsed, which is excellently dramatized in Epie Ngome's allegorical drama piece, also finds echoes in MacViban's poetry. Ngome's *What God Has Put Asunder* shows the genesis of the conflict between Francophone Cameroon and Anglophone Cameroon to have started at reunification which was conducted without the genuine consent of Weka (Anglophone). The failure of the union can therefore be found in its very dubious and manipulative inception. In the poem "Exodus" which uses biblical allusions to communicate the experience of the liberation of British Southern Cameroons from the colonial yoke of Britain, the poet evokes the image of a "vague dream" to describe the union with French Cameroon. The persona says:

> Out went we, with flocks and herds
> Out of Pharaoh's custody, seeking
> The Promised Land. Songs of deliverance
> Rose from griots and gongs –
> Tore the air with liberation-lyrics.
> Our marriage— now a vague dream—
> Was some distant lore of how
> WE LIVED IN DEATH. (14)

The biblical story of the liberation of the people of Israel from the tyranny of the Egyptian king Pharaoh is artistically employed to talk about the liberation of the peoples of Southern Cameroons from colonial rule and their eventual union with the already independent French Cameroon. "We" in the context of the story that is being translated here refers to the Israelite, and in the context of the poem it refers to Anglophone Cameroon or better still Southern Cameroon, to place it in the right historical frame. The "Promised Land" is far from being the "land of promise" and "land of glory" that is sung in the Cameroon national anthem. It is not a destination or location as expressed in the biblical story of Exodus. It is more of a state of mind - the condition of freedom that comes with independence; the possibility and beauty of self-rule and making choices that reflect the people's values without recurs to a colonial authority. This condition or state of mind is reflected in the "Songs of deliverance / Rose from griots and gongs – / Tore the air with liberation-lyrics" (14) as the people listened to, trusted and believed the political ideologies of the leading politicians - "Marching to the tune of the prophet's voice –" (14). The poet equates the position of the politician to that of a prophet thereby making the prophet a politician. Moses in the story of Exodus thus occupies the office of a prophet and a politician and politicians like Endeley and Foncha who championed the different courses of Southern Cameroon liberation share such dual functions. As politicians they wanted control of the issues of their people, as prophets they defined the vision and the ideologies that were to guide the people as they fought for liberation from British rule. It was one of such ideologies, particularly that of John Ngu Foncha, that brought about the union between French Cameroon and Southern Cameroons, which the poet laments to have been "some distant lore of how / WE LIVED IN DEATH" (14). Independence for the Southern Cameroons was therefore not a birth but death; it was not the beginning of a new nation but another, even more severe, dimension of colonial subjugation. Piet Konings and Francis Nyamjoh point out in "Construction and Deconstruction" that:

> contrary to Anglophone expectations upon reunification, federalism, far from providing for

> equal partnership between Anglophones and Francophones and guaranteeing cultural continuity for the former, turned out to be nothing more than a comma in a long sentence of assimilation of the Anglophone minority. (12)

This is why the poet thinks that marriage was a nebulous delusion which told tales of how the people were moving from one form of death to another severe form.

Another fundamental aspect which reveals the punctured relationship between the two Cameroons is expressed in "Waiting for The Dawn"; a beautifully crafted poem that plays with the notion of time as a delicate yet awkward concept that acts upon the faith of the subjugated Anglophone providing both instances of dire despair and over-powering hope. As the title suggests, one of the central images in the poem is that of "dawn" and the dominant concept is that of time and the tides it brings which is embodied in the term "Waiting". The title of the poem is closely associated to Oscar C. Labang's "Waiting for a Declaration" in which the poet professes deep expectations about a declaration that could end the long years of suppression of the Cameroonian people. Both poems build on the notion of waiting and the hope for some form of change. The first stanza of the poem opens strategically with an onomatopoeic device as one imagines "Sounds" piercing through the quietude of the night. The experiences associated with the sound and the night is horrifying especially in relation to what the Anglophone undergoes. The themes of belonging and alienation are paradoxical extremes that capture the misery of living in such complexity. This is evident in the following:

> Sounds too often pierce the night
> Of belonging and alienation, both inchoate here
> Long's the wait— the sun must break
> The night's back. Will you be too blind
> To see the light like cavemen, or
> Run to the horizon of a new day?
> Many a vain dawn have I seen
> Whose smile soon faded away— false alarm, alas.
> We have chased off the heavens
> And now sit cloudless
> But the moon has helped us with
> Our harvest, O moon (15)

The sound is suggestive of the trauma that goes through the mind of the Anglophones as they imagine or wait for dawn. The trauma, evoked by the duality of "belonging and alienation" that cohabit in the consciousness defines the problematic personality of the speaker in a cycle of waiting. The question of belonging has far more profound meaning and implication to the Anglophone and it seems to have been enshrined in the cultural mentality of the people. Piet Konings and Francis Nyamjoh point out that the issue has also been at the centre of the division amongst Anglophones. They write:

> The 1996 constitution and the politics of belonging in the 1990s might have institutionalised and intensified the sense of divisions among Anglophones, but this by no means implies that the Machiavellian designs of the Francophone-dominated state for asphyxiating Anglophone identity started then. (12)

The notion therefore has been politicized and made to breed division among Anglophones. This possibly is why the poet thinks that Anglophones exist in the paradox of belonging and alienation. The idea of waiting in the poem is also a source of trauma because the persona has been waiting for too long. The image of the cave resurfaces as the persona tries to situate his position in the light of the darkness of dawn. The possibility of the rejection to see the light, expressed in a rhetorical question, correlates with the "false alarm" or the "vain dawn" that gives the persona false hopes and then vanishes before he can fully come to terms with it. The transference of quality from humans to the dawn, which is said to be smiling, expresses in a convincing way the ephemeral nature or brevity of the hope that soon fades. The dominance of images of light – "sun", "light" and "moon" – is a pointer of the possibilities of hope for a people who have been waiting for too long in a world described in terms of darkness and night. Emphatic optimism comes to focus when the speaker talks about the long wait and the fact that "the sun must break" even as darkness threatens to come back.

The centrality of time both in itself and as a moment of the day "dawn", and the idea of waiting are particularly relevant in the consciousness of a marginalized people as they continually hope that a new day or the passage of time will bring some form of change to their experience.

> Time — a dangerous concept, full of tricks
> I've been here before, not knowing
> Who and what and where I am (15)

The tricky nature of time stems from the fact that it has led the speaker to some point in his struggle that he does not have complete knowledge of himself, or the values he stands for or the place where he is. Time is a cyclical concept because the journey through time has brought the speaker back to a condition where he has once been and he can recognize that: "I've been here before". The "here" in this line does not serve the mere grammatical role of an adverb of place; it expresses a value or condition that is more complex and profound in experience. It could refer to a strategic stage in the suffering of the individual or his people; it could also refer to a point in time and space during which the speaker encountered a particular experience…; it could as well refer to a moment of epiphany during which the poet thought he would come to greater self-awareness but he ended up not knowing anything.

Within the frame of time, therefore, "here" can become anything beyond a location or point of reference.

Although time is considered a tricky phenomenon that plays on the sensibilities and perceptions, the poet still believes that it is only time that can turn the fortune of the speaker and his people. It has the potential of giving the people a new vision or of fulfilling the vision they already have. This redeeming potential of time and the vision that the poet hopes will come to fulfilment at some point in the cycle of time are communicated in the following stanza:

> Time is still— some necromancer's trick
> But we all know "some day for sure"
> The harvest of thorns will give way
> And we'll be flooded with a harvest of plenty.
> We wish only to rebuild, is that
> Too much to ask…?
> We wish only to rebuild the fragments
> Of a second Divide and Rule. (16)

The image of a "harvest of thorns" discussed earlier reappears in this stanza and still bears a message of bitterness and frustration. But unlike in the earlier instances the image is contrasted with "a harvest of plenty" which will be greater than ever imagine "flood". Time is expected to result in positive change – from and experience of thorns to one of plenty. There is a deeper conviction; a more enshrined sense of surety about the possibility of change. It is the poet's hope that this change in fate will be accompanied by wishes to "rebuild the fragments / Of a second Divide and Rule" (16).

Dzekashu MacViban in *Scions of the Malcontent* communicates a vision that is central to the understanding of the complex relationship between Anglophones and Francophones in the postcolonial Cameroon nation. He is part of the artistic community that uses poetry as, to use the words of Oscar C. Labang, "a tool for the regulation of human relations - with themselves, with their community, with their leaders, and with the powers that control their universe" ("Introduction", i). The poetry of MacViban shows that he is committed to addressing the issues that affect his nation or that animate life in his society. The poet holds the conviction that Cameroon as a nation was founded on a false premise, and the marginalization of one part by the other is evidence of the betrayal of the terms on which the nation was founded.

CHAPTER SEVEN
"DREAMS FOR TOMORROW": SYMBOLS OF HOPE AND UNITY IN GWEDENG NGALAH'S *THE OLIVE TREE*

Cameroon poetry in English depends heavily on symbolism with many poets stepping out of the conventional convenience of poetic symbols to create new individual symbols or use conventional symbols in new and quizzical ways. A symbol is a person, object, image, word, or event that evokes and conveys a range of additional meaning beyond and usually more abstract than its literal significance. It is an educational device used to evoke complex ideas without having to resort to painstaking explanations. Symbolism is an aspect of what F.V.N. Painter calls artistic element when he says "there is an artistic element in literature upon which the value of any work largely depends. The art is in the choice and marshalling of words". Conventional symbols have meanings that are widely recognized by a society or culture. Although poets use conventional symbols to reinforce meanings, symbols sometimes go beyond their conventional symbolism. A specific context determines the symbolic meaning of different objects, events, ideas and words.

Gwedeng Ngalah is one of the most prolific aestheticians in Anglophone Cameroon poetry. A first glance at his poetry is likely to create a false impression that he is more concerned with aesthetic twists than with the crucial issues rocking the nation. Ngalah's prowess as a poet, therefore, lies in his ability to weave themes that are central to his people and to humankind with fine imaginative and inventive playfulness. This chapter is based on the premise that in some of his poems Ngalah manipulates a series of symbols to convey a message of hope and unity for the Cameroon nation. It is interesting and somewhat intriguing to read an Anglophone Cameroon poet writing about hope and calling for a united Cameroon at a time when the general tendency is to castigate the status-quo and call for a political revolution that gives Anglophones a more central place in the nation. Like Shadrach Ambanasom in his collection *Homage and Courtship*, Ngalah is against the general current of thought in Anglophone Cameroon poetry. This however does not in any way suggest a sense of escapism from the political hotspots of the society. Rather, it shows that the poetry is not only a harangue of satire and revolution but also a means of pointing to positive directions at a time when everything in the nation seems weird. At moments of crisis or loss poetry can offer a decisive way of fixing the meaning, importance and influence of the events and objects. In a typical modernist style, Ngalah's poetry picks objects, ideas and events that hitherto would not be considered relevant for poetic art, and out of them convey multiple layers of meaning, one of which is hope for a united and harmonious Cameroon nation.

One of Ngalah's finest poems is "Dreams for Tomorrow"; the verse is firmer and the speaker combines symbols of a river, marriage and cordiality to drive across the vision of unity which he perceives to be the fate of Cameroon. Major symbols in the poem are the "River Mungo", the "nuptial bliss" and the idea of "die to rise again". The Mungo River is the historic river that marks a boundary line between East and West Cameroon. It has been used variously in Cameroon literature most particularly either to symbolize unity or separation. The collapse of the bridge over this river was interpreted by many anti-unification individuals as a symbol of the collapse of the bond that ties the two nations together. In this poem, it is used as a symbol of unending unity which according to the poet dies only to rise again in "candid love and peace". The three stanza poem in its entirety with the graphic representation goes thus:

> Rolling softy into the Atlantic,
> Into the vast ocean where two states blend
> Varied cultures drowned in wild deeps as
> East and west in nuptial bliss do die to

Rise again, ruled by candid love and peace.

Myriad voices ring in one subtle note
Under thy solid bridge that sustains this
Nation with two states, bound by faith and hope,
Glowing with bright light of a golden Star
On which we rest our dreams for tomorrow.

The river gives another mythical significance to the relationship between the English and French speaking sections of the nation. Rivers can be symbolic of a journey; physical, emotional, or spiritual. The union of the Cameroons is therefore a journey with physical, emotional and spiritual ramifications. The river is a melting point of all the different culture of Cameroon and it carries the fate and faith of the two states and strolls "softly" into the Atlantic. The ocean is a mystical and mythical entity which signifies among many other things the mystery of life. It is a place of limitlessness and when standing on its shores, the ocean appears to stretch into eternity. Its depth and breadth represent deep emotions. The fact that the Mungo River is personified, as it is said to be "strolling", suggests that the movement of the river is intimately related to the peoples it links. The significations of Rivers and Seas can generally be better understood if they are accompanied by descriptive words because they can be both savage and redemptive. The poet's choice of words here plays a very central role in revealing what he thinks and wants to establish as the role of the river/sea in the unity of the Cameroon nation. Apart from the use of gerund "strolling" which symbolizes the leisurely manner with which the river flows, there is also the use of the adverb "softly". This suggests calm and rhythmic movement which symbolizes a relaxed state of being, movement characterized by being in touch with your intuition, or of being in harmony with the universe. The submersion of the many cultures of Cameroon does not create any disruption in the movement of the river; rather the river accepts all of these and carries them gently and smoothly into the ocean. The fact that the poet gets the "Varied cultures drowned in wild deeps" suggests that the union is an act that is irreversible, irretrievable and irrevocable.

The use of nuptial symbolism to illustrate the union between Southern Cameroons and La Republique is not new in Anglophone Cameroon writing. The image has been elaborately explored by Victor Epie Ngome in his interesting allegorical play with the ironic title *What God Has Put Asunder*. The difference, however, is that why Epie Ngome and others use this image to reveal the marginalization of one partner in the marriage and thus the need for divorce. Contrary to many writers who use such nuptial symbolism to suggest the need for separation, Ngalah uses this image to show that the union is eternal whether for good or ill. The idea is conveyed through the vision of dying and rising again which suggests an experience that is similar to that of the ancient Egyptian Phoenix bird. In ancient Egypt and in classical antiquity, the phoenix was a fabulous bird with brilliant scarlet and gold plumage and a melodious cry. Only one phoenix existed at a time, and it was very long-lived. As its death approached, the phoenix fashioned a nest of aromatic boughs and spices, which the sun set on fire and the bird consumed in the flames. From the pyre a new phoenix sprang miraculously. The phoenix was thus associated with immortality and the allegory of resurrection and life after death (*Dictionary of Mythology*). By employing the mythic idea of dying and resurrecting, the poet brings to mind the fact that there can be only one Cameroon nation and it would live eternally. It is a lot more interesting when the poet thinks that it will not simply rise again but will rise in a new spirit; one controlled by love and peace.

Ngalah's poems are a lot more interesting when they are quoted in their entirety because they give the stylistic double titling and repetition of the title in the last line of the poems. There is the main title and an alternative title and the main title is often repeated in the last line of the poem. This double titling is made evident through the bolding and capitalization of the title and the initial letters of each line of verse. Reading the capitalized initials vertically from top to bottom gives RIVER MUNGO. This alternative title gives a clue to the central idea in the poem especially when correlated with the main title. The central idea in this poem is the eternal unity of the two Cameroons as symbolized by the Mungo River and the bridge that links both states. It is in this river that the fate of both states "varied cultures" is submerged in a nuptial union. The bond of this eternal unity in the vision of the poet lies in the Mungo River in which "myriad voices ring in one subtle note" beneath the bridge that holds the two Cameroons together in a union of "faith and hope" led by a golden star to "dreams of tomorrow". All the cultures have been merged in the unitary "Star" which is another symbol in the poem. The star is so unique and important that it is spelled with a capital "S" in the middle of a sentence. The "Star" embodies both the unitary star on the flag of Cameroon and the symbol of hope that the poet seeks to communicate in the entire poem.

The message of rising for love and peace in "Dreams of Tomorrow" is taken up again in "Uniting for Peace". This poem is dedicated to the United Republic of Cameroon. This is the Cameroon that was born from the pyre or ashes of the Federal Republic of Cameroon following the memorandum of 1972. History has it that it was the need to tighten his role and the fear of ethnic conflict that led President Amadou Ahidjo to concentrate power in his hands by

abolishing the Federal system and renaming the country the United Republic of Cameroon. The speaker in this poem seems to be in accord with the president's move as the poem is a meditation on peace and "mutual good" as the sole essence for which the United Republic of Cameroon existed. According to the speaker:
> Uniting for peace breeds bliss when true love
> Neutralizes doubts in men's mind to prove
> Intrinsic bond between two states that seek to renew
> Their battered dreams in one sleek
> Existence and so foster the progress
> Designed to pave the path to her greatness. (22)

The poet's vision is conveyed through the use of phrases like "uniting for peace", "intrinsic bond", "renew/Their battered dreams in one sleek/ Existence" and "pave the path to her greatness". The dreams in "Dreams for Tomorrow" is defined here as battered dreams. The dreams which the poet continually evoke are symbols of the horror that Cameroonians have lived for decades of separation and loveless brotherhood. The dreams have been battered by years and decades of accusation and counter accusation, suspicion and insult but the poet thinks that it is time to renew the "battered dreams" and transform them into a smooth existence that reveals the greatness of the nation and its people. He reveals the beauty of reuniting when the speaker says:
> Reuniting, thus, is glorious since peace

Ensures that men and women know the bliss
Patriotic parents prayed should last for long
Under the influence of love that stays strong
Beyond the superficial smile that soon
Loses its lustre before a new moon
Is born to reveal the false gleam behind
Creamy clouds that veil the gloom in the mind:

Reuniting the French and English Cameroons according to the poet is a fulfilment of the wish of the founding fathers of the nation. The alliterative /p/ in "Patriotic parents prayed" is a plosive that shows the force with which the poet articulates his vision of unity. The poet acknowledges the existence of falsehood "superficial smile" hidden by "creamy clouds". But he thinks that the "love that stays strong" can surpass hatred and division because such negative values "soon / Loses its lustre before a new moon". The poet believes strongly in love that is sincere because

Only true love can reason how such gloom
Frees two states from bondage that made them bloom.

Coming, thus, together for mutual good
Assures a boom to come in form of flood
Meant to drown our drear doubts and fears as we
Engage to build new paradise to be
Reflective of the sublime vows we take
Only to ensure the efforts we make
Open up new routes for the progress of

National unity with love enough.

The bondage of Anglophone Cameroon in the union with French Cameroon has been emphasized in almost all spheres of academic disciplines. Writers in all genres have repeatedly evoked the problem with some opting for cessation. Ngalah's take on the subject is somewhat interesting and absorbing. In as much as he acknowledges that there is bondage, he thinks that true love transforms the gloom of bondage into a bloom. The poet is highly positive and takes a lot of poetic effort to convey his positivity. Ngalah's insistence on the necessity to love in the face of problems is reminiscent of W.H. Auden's famous lines on the need for love in a world confronted with existential frustration. In the poem September 11, 1939, Auden in the last but one stanza writes:

> And no one exists alone;
> Hunger allows no choice
> To the citizen or the police;
> We must love one another or die.

Like Auden, Ngalah thinks that one Cameroon cannot exist alone; the two parts must coexist because both parts face some similar challenges. Confronted with these challenges or inequalities, the only option that can bring sanity is love. So much in the same line with Auden, Ngalah thinks that the two Cameroons must love each other to be able to build a solid nation. The dream which the poet communicates is grounded in the future. His mind is focused not on his present condition but on how love can be nurtured so that the future will be great. Uniting for the good of one another brings a "boom" that will come like a "flood". The flood is a symbol of the overwhelming quantity or volume of good that can be reaped from unity and equity. The flood therefore is a powerful symbol that drives home the benefits of unity in an alarming and awesome way. It will overpower the fear and dreariness that prevent the people from engaging in the building of a great and united postcolonial Cameroon nation.

Ngalah uses football as a symbolic force that pulls Cameroonians into one spirit of nationhood and nationalism. This game is a source of hope to the people that there is still something that all Cameroonians, keeping aside tribal, linguistic and regional differences can believe in and share national pride about. This vision is expressed in two separate poems all of which have to do with football. In the two stanza poem dedicated to the Indomitable Lions, the national football team of Cameroon, he sees each victory of the team as a moment for fraternal brotherhood. The speaker says:

> In the swiftness of two dozen legs on a pitch
> National Unity assumes a fresher meaning:
> Diverse voices in various tongues arise to sing
> ONE Song of ONE Victory for ONE Nation,
> Moved by the singular spirit of sportsmanship
> Ingrained in our rich cultural heritage. (44)

> The rhythm of the tam tam will reverberate at dusk
> And the ringing bells chime in the moon's brightness
> Before a new dawn's slanting arrows prick out
> Loyalty and love for this great Triangle in the
> Exuberant display of songs and dance of victory.
> (44)

The football skills of the players "swiftness of two dozen legs" redefine the notion of national unity by giving it a "fresher meaning" emphasized through the capitalization of the initial letters in "National Unity". The poet explains the new meaning in the four lines that follow the colon at the end of the second line. This new meaning is brought about by the fact that the entire nation celebrates the victory of the team. The image of different voices in varied tongues symbolizes the linguistic diversity of Cameroon, which has often been a source of conflict both at the national and regional levels. The fact that these conflicting tongues come together to sing a common song of victory means that football is a uniting force. To stress on the oneness that football victory generates among the diverse peoples, the poet adopts the techniques of capitalization and repetition. In the line "ONE Song of ONE Victory for ONE Nation", there is the unusual capitalization of the word "ONE" as well as the initial of other words within the line of verse. These, together with the repetition of ONE thrice create a sense of emphasis or insistence. While the other words "Song",

"Victory" and "Nation" are important and emphasized, the ONE is over emphasized through complete capitalization and repetition as every other word takes its meaning from one.

The poet's idea therefore is to call attention to the oneness that Cameroonians share each time the national team gains victory. Such victories are characterized by singing and dancing. The tam tam and the bell are representations of celebration as they produce the music to which the people dance for victory. The expression "Loyalty and love for this great Triangle" is a demonstration of the allegiance that Cameroonians have for the nation. The triangle is an imagistic representation of the geographical structure of Cameroon with its sharp North and broad South structure. The pride of this nation is revived through the fame of the players:

> Luminary of African and World Football
> In the glowing flame of your global fame
> Our national pride is rekindled as
> Now we all wait in great expectation to
> Sing again and again our National Song of Victory.
> (44)

According to the poet, the nation derives pride in Africa and around the world as well as national unity and cohesion thanks to the football ability of the national team. This is a corroboration of the opinions of some political figures who use the victories of the football team as grounds for discussions on issues of national integration and patriotism. This tendency to see in the victory of the Indomitable Lions as a vision of a united Cameroon with patriotic citizens has been castigated by football critics and commentators like Sam Nuvala Fonkem who thinks that the celebration of football victories is an expression of mere sentimentalism and fanfarism than patriotism. He posits in the article "Cameroon/Egypt: Snapshot - Pharaoh, Let My People Go!" that:

> Selfless attachment to the fatherland is the real stuff of which patriotism is made and not the ephemeral excitement and pleasure derived from kicking or watching a team kick on a pitch. Patriotism is made of sterner stuff; sterner than the fluffy sentimentalism, fanfarism and fanaticism that have impacted on the Cameroonian psyche and elevated football on a religious pedestal. (Par. 4)

He thinks that it is not only misleading but deceitful to depend on the excitement from football victories as a measurement of patriotism and national unity. He further argues that:

> The tendency to equate the successes of the Indomitable Lions with the deplorable socio-economic and political performance of Cameroon has been very misleading, deceitful and illogical. The tendency to misconstrue the image of an ad hoc football team as a symbol of national cohesion, unity and stability distorts the true sentiments on which genuine patriotism is founded. (Par. 3)

Fonkem, thus thinks that success in a football pitch does not in any way relate to questions of patriotism because patriotism is measured through what he describes as "sterner stuff" a phrase which suggests more serious issues. While Fonkem thinks that football victory is not "sterner stuff", Ngalah thinks that it is an avenue that rallies the people to one course. It gives them reason to celebrate as well as to embrace each other without regard of language, culture or ethnic origin. A similar expression of unity and celebration derived from sports can be seen in the film *Invictus* which tells the story of how Nelson Mandela used the baseball game to erase sentiments of hatred and antagonism among the South African racial groups. At the time when it is believed that blacks will set out on a scheme of revenge because they have just taken political power in South Africa, Invictus (the President) works against the segregationist thoughts and actions of his party cohorts and manages to unite his people through sports – baseball. This show of unity is manifested most strikingly between his body guards. When the baseball team wins the world cup, a black guard and a white guard who have been suspicious and antagonistic towards each other finally smile and embrace themselves. Even before the victory of the team, the President watches through his window how his guards, blacks and whites, are playing baseball together at the back of the presidency. Like,

Invictus in the film, Ngalah envisions Cameroonians celebrating football victories amidst ancestral drums "tam tam" and forgetting the wounds of antagonism that we have long inflicted on each other.

The Federation of Cameroon Football is the focus of another poem which employs football symbolism to convey a message of hope for a united Cameroon. In "What We Owe Football", the poet says that football is a source of pride which all citizens share and would not want bureaucrats to destroy it. He writes:

> **F**ootball remains the pride of this country
> **E**very citizen would not want to see
> **D**estroyed by selfish interest bureaucrats
> **E**mploy to thwart the zeal in technocrats
> **R**eady to restore national prestige
> **A**s set by prim patriots who did not breach
> **T**he solemn contract signed and sealed with blood
> **I**n which today we swim as in a flood
> **O**f victories that drowns all hostile forces
> **N**ow entering to drain our rich resources. (43)

Football to the poet is a means of restoring national prestige and giving the people and the nation a source of oneness. The poet expresses the wish that bureaucrats should not step in to disrupt the enthusiasm of "technocrats" who are ready to maintain the spirit of patriotism initiated by the nation's forefathers in the act of losing their blood for the nation: "The solemn contract signed and sealed with blood". The conception of the fight for independence as a bond sealed with blood can be better understood if it is read within the context of the Cameroon National Anthem especially the opening stanza where the lyrics read: "O Cameroon, Thou Cradle of our Fathers, / Holy Shrine where in our midst they now repose, / Their tears and blood and sweat thy soil did water". The poet refers to the "our Father" as "prim patriots". In his opinion, the players "technocrats" of the national team are ready to continue this patriotic spirit and that is why "Over this globe our flag soars because / Football binds us all in one cogent cause" (43). Football is a convincing ground for the restoration of national pride revealed in the metaphor of the flag soaring over the globe.

The poet's vision of football as a basis for national unity is expressed more forcefully in the third stanza of the poem. In this stanza, he comes out clearly and states that what we owe the game of football is that collective struggle "to rise and never fall / As one nation". Football has given the nation a reason to engage in a communal struggle for national unity:

> Communal strife to rise and never to fall
> As one nation is what we owe football
> Modeled against selfish interest that kill
> Enthusiasm and thus weaken the thrill
> Reuniting us in one strong spirit
> Of love and loyalty without limit,
> Orchestrated by rich diversity

Nature nurtures to reap prosperity. (43)

Like in the first stanza, there is a lingering fear that some egoistic attitude can ruin the courage of the citizens and the players. In the first stanza, mention is made of bureaucrats that thwart the passion of technocrats and here again there is "selfish interest that kill[s]". However, in both instances the desire of the citizens is given an edge over the interest of individuals. Communal struggle to rise and never fall is "[m]odeled against selfish interest" and football becomes a factor that reunites Cameroonians in a spirit of love and limitless loyalty.

The poet however cautions that if the uniting influence of football has to be sustained then everybody needs to do something – promote and preserve "order and true peace". He says:

> For such progress to be sustained
> Order and true peace need to be maintained
> On all by all foe all who seek to lead
> This nation that sees in soccer a seed
> Breeding to spread the fine fruit of success
> Achieving on pitch of play to prick progress
> Loyal subjects will hail when we mount high
> Like the same flag each victory sets to fly (43)

Each person who sees football as a means of bringing progress needs to participate in making this dream true by offering order and peace to others. Everybody should be considered as equal citizen of one nation with equal pride and rights. In this way the seed of football will be able to bear fruits of success.

There is the dominant use of alliterative phrases and rhyming couplets throughout the poem. The sounds and meanings of the words combine to create a mood beyond the readers' fun to read and pleasure to hear. In the first stanza there are phrases like "ready to restore" and "prim patriots" with the repeated /r/ and /p/ sounds that seems to convey the patriots readiness to restore the nations pride; in the second stanza there is "love and loyalty without limits" and "Nature nurtures" and in the third stanza there is "fine fruit" and "pitch of play to prick progress. The rhyme follows the tradition of rhyming couplets in an aa bb cc dd ee ff gg pattern. In the first stanza "country" in line one rhyme with "see" in line two. The rhyme in these two words is produced by the short /I/ vowel sound. In similar light the ultimate segment of sounds in "bureaucrats" sound the same with "technocrats" in the following line. The phonetic rendition of the bureaucrats and the rendition of technocrats show that the last syllable /krats/ in both words are rendered the same. This sound segment especially the combination of the /k/, /r/ and /a/ produces a crashing effect which somewhat suggest the crushing of the zeal of technocrats by bureaucrats which as the poet says is something the citizens do not want to see. The same rhyme pattern applies to "prestige and breach", "blood and flood" and "forces and resources" in the first stanza and in the others. In some cases only single phonetic sounds rhyme, in others there are sound segments that produce the rhyme. The many alliterative phrases and the rhyming couplets give the poem a melody that blends with the poet's pleasant vision of football as a source of inspiration for national prestige and unity.

Placed within the context of Cameroonian football in recent years and within the historical period during which the poems were written, one may be tempted to think that the poet is an over-zealous optimist. This standpoint emerges from the consciousness that, for some years, football has increasingly served both as a source of division and sectionalism and an avenue where individualistic bureaucratic manifestations have found expression. While it is true that Cameroonian Football and/or footballers have a world-wide fan-following and that this has been proven many a time on the global stage, one wonders whether this game in recent years has attracted the same zeal and support from Cameroonians as it did say during the 90s. The poem "National Song of Victory" dedicated to the national football team, Indomitable Lions was written in August 2005. It is worth noting that the team finished in the second place in the 2003 FIFA Confederations cup, in 2004 this team was knocked out at the quarter-finals in the African Nations Cup and in 2005 (the year the poem was written) it did not qualify for the Confederations cup. This makes the poet's use of the team as a source of vision for hard work, national unity and oneness problematic. The second poem in this line "What we owe Football" written in 2007 and dedicated to the Federation of Cameroon Football also leave much to desire as far as its message is concerned. Two years before this poem was written, Football brought no special attention to the nation and attracted very little interest from the citizens as the football team got knocked-out of the African Nations Cup for two consecutive seasons (2004 and 2006). In 2005, it failed to qualify for the Confederations Cup and failed to qualify for the Germany World Cup adventure in 2006. These continuous failures are indications that the "technocrats" whom the poet talks about in the first stanza of the poem have lost the sense of national pride. Between 2002 and 2006, Cameroon did not have any victory after being unable to win any of the next three African Cups and failing to qualify for the 2006 FIFA World cup. The team is an ailing lion on an almost permanent downturn in achievement. Consequently, there is much to wonder regarding how a game and a team that has consistently brought shame (failure) to the nation can be emblematic of national pride or an inspiration for national unity as expressed in "What we owe Football", and in making the people to celebrate in "ONE Song of ONE Victory of ONE Nation" as expressed in "National Song of Victory".

In spite of the lack of realistic details about the condition of the team at the time the poems were written, there is an aura of achievement from past exploits that still gives the nation value and recognition in the international scene. Hilarious Ambe in an article titled "The Anglophone-Francophone Marriage and Anglophone Dramatic Compositions in the Cameroon Republic" published in 2004 captures the essence of football and the pride it can bring in the following anecdote:

> Quite recently, I was at a conference in Leipzig, and during one of the coffee breaks, I found myself in a conversation with a group of other participants. When I introduced myself as a Cameroonian, two of the persons in our little group exclaimed, almost at the same time: "Ha! Roger Milla! Football!" I simply nodded with a grin, somehow proud that almost a decade after Cameroon's ace football striker—Roger Milla's wonderful performance at the World Cup Football Finals in Italia 90, my country was still being remembered and praised. (71)

Ambe is testifying to the power of football to place the nation on the international stage for positive recognition. I have had two similar experiences at a supermarket in 2010 and hospital in 2012 in Kansas

City (USA) where the moment I mentioned that I am from Cameroon, the American and Asian with whom I was talking immediately make reference to Roger Milla and Samuel Eto'o Fils respectively. Although no football fan in the real sense of the word, I felt a certain degree of importance about football and my nation. For once, I was not asked "what is Cameroon?" or "where is that at?" I suddenly realized that football had given the nation a degree of fame compared only to that which corruption has also infamously propelled it. This is evidence that even while the nation is caught in spasms of confusion on how to reconcile the Football federation and the team/players, the nation continues to enjoy relative international recognition for the exploits of its players either as individuals or as a team.

The poet also makes use of religious symbolism to be able to push across his vision. The biblical world of harmony and fulfilment – the Garden of Eden, is used to reflect the position or type of existence that should characterize the nation. The poem is entitled "Eden on Earth" and the side title is "West and East Cameroon". This establishes a link between the Eden which the poet envisions on earth and the two sides of Cameroon. "Eden on Earth" thus is a call for Cameroonians to consider the union between the West and the East as a treasure that must be held with care and pride because it gives the country its uniqueness.

We killed all private fears in us when we
Entered the pact sealed with light of one bright
Star that takes the central throne on red and
Two leave green to make brothers live one joy

as artificial bridges of alien
nomination die in the birth of one
destined to bind our common traditions.

Eternal union remains for us, now,
A sterling treasure to behold as one
State is made haven for cultural wealth
To be named Africa in miniature.

Commonwealth and Francophonie find now
A common bed to rest conflicting quests
Made one in this triangular sea where
Elysian bliss doth freely flow to spread
Round the globe, uniting people in states
Of varied customs and tastes that depend
On this peaceful wedlock of cultures for
Nations to bury all strife in one love
So our world is made an Eden on Earth.

The star and the colours red and green in the first stanza are symbols that are recurrent in Ngalah's poetry. He continually draws from the repertoire of Cameroon national symbols to express the idea of the need for unity. The star and colours are all part of the Cameroon national flag. By borrowing from a collection of recognizable symbols and by repeating them over and again, the poet succeeds first in calling the attention of Cameroonians to the relevance of their national symbols and second in re-reading the meaning of these symbols to the people. Conscious of the power that poetry has on the mind, it can be said that the poet is in a struggle to revoke the significance of these symbols in the consciousness of the Cameroonian people. These symbols are intended to make the people to "kill all private fears". These fears were killed when the two states opted to become one nation. It is evident however that these fears have over time resurfaced and so the poet thinks that by re-evoking these symbols he can call "brothers (to) live one joy".

The Eden symbol reappears in the third stanza through the idea of a "haven for cultural wealth" with genuine treasures that combine to make the nation "Africa in miniature". The unity of Cameroon is a treasure not only for Cameroonians but also for international organizations like Francophonie and Commonwealth which use it as a place for the mishmash of their ideological differences. The example of brotherhood / nationhood in Cameroon will inspire other peoples around the world to "bury all strife in one love" so that the world can become an Eden. The poet's insistence on love of one another as the bases for communal existence gives his message a universal appeal. The only possibility for a meaningful co-existence is therefore based on love. The idea of love, like the use of national symbols, is recurrent in the poetry of Ngalah and it resonates with the poet's hope and vision of unity and acceptance.

This is the duty of the poet; this is where the visionary power of the poet comes to focus; this is where sublime essence blends with artistic intuition to communicate what lies beyond the vision of those who have not the power to enter into higher visionary realms. The poet speaks better to a nation when they see their values declining and cannot believe in the things that have provided mirth and hope over time.

The tenor of the discussion here brings us to the place where the discussion began - that Ngalah communicates his vision of a united Cameroon nation through the manipulation of different symbols at different instances in his poetry. He artistically re-evokes classical, conventional and national symbols to persuade Cameroonians to see the union of the two states as an opportunity to explore and make life meaningful and worthwhile. What makes Ngalah a poet that is different from other Anglophone Cameroonian poets is his ability to pick the objects, events, names and ideas directly and clearly without tainting them yet making such arty twists that give everything a new and refreshing outlook.

CHAPTER EIGHT
EXORCIZING THE NATION: SEARCH FOR DIVINE INTERVENTION IN JOHN NGONGKUM NGONG'S *WALLS OF AGONY*

John Ngongkum Ngong in his poetry seeks to harmonise the wild history of human civilization characterised by evil, greed and immorality with mythic reality through a horizon of spirituality. The interaction with the realm of deities forms an integral part of the African poet's cosmo-poetic consciousness and reveals the functional dynamics of myth, mystery and reliance on supreme forces. In the poetry of John Ngongkum Ngong, this is manifested in "a constant appeal to spiritual essence to provide the poet with 'wisdom, brush and paint' with which he yearns to reconstruct the universe flawed with evil" (Nkengasong, 11). The poet's dependence on the spiritual essence is an expression of a universal African value. The poet returns to spirituality and myth to derive wholesomeness in the face of chaos and evil. This chapter analyses the poetry of John Ngongkum Ngong to show that the poet communes with deities and transcends the supreme zone of the sacred in order to derive power to rebuild his society. His poetry thus is a tool for reconstructing the frail walls of the nation that he sees as crumbling.

In "Powerless", the poet acknowledges his impotency to carry out the divine mission assigned to him. This acknowledgement goes along with the recognition of the source of his poetic power - Kezeh. He says:

> I know I am powerless
> And fragile like a dry gourd
> Here where lizards legislate.
> Power I know is Kezeh's possession
> Yet the uncircumcised burn of their fingers
> Preparing a fire for my ghetto. (31)

The invocation of the poet's powerlessness is made more vivid when it is associated to a "dry gourd". His fragility is compared to the frailness of a dry climber tendril. The gourd is also the shell of the fruit dried and excavated for use as a water bottle, float or rattle. It is very fragile and gets easily broken once it is not handled with care. The poet or his poetic vision is fragile and does not need to be tempered with. The fragility of the poet is however situated within the "Here" that is, a particular context. It is a context where reptiles are legislators. The artistic verve in the phrase "lizards legislate" does not spring only from the alliterative use of the /l/ sound but more from the image of the Lizard collocated to legislators.

The "Lizard" is a symbol of the jungle system and the celebration of mediocrity. The society thus is a "duncedom". Dunces are people who show no capacity for learning, dullards or blocked headed yet they are the ones who dominate in the poet's society. This is a clear conveyance of the idea that the mediocre are given undue positions possibly because of their tribal leanings or origin. The speaker says:

> I hunger to blossom
> Decked in freedom garments.
> Here where dunces dominate.
> Sipping the palm wine of our sweat
> I hunger to flourish
> Rooted in genuine love
> Where tribalism commands
> Munching the heart of competence. (31)

Even though the poet acknowledges that he is powerless, he has a strong desire to soar above the evil that is ruining the nation. The principal evils enunciated upon are mediocrity, embezzlement and tribalism. The negative effect of this is revealed in the personification in which tribalism is said to be "munching the hearts of competence". In this tribalistic context the poet as a moral visionary desires to blossom or to "flourish", that is to live above the evil and corruption of his immediate society. Embezzlement is highlighted in the phrase "sipping the palm wine of pour sweat" (31). People who do not deserve it consume the labour of the masses.

The powerlessness of the poet is in relation to the problem in his society. He seems to be insignificant in the face of the mass evil confronting his people but his recognition that power is Kezeh's possession is a step towards obtaining the power that he needs to combat evil. This recognition is derived from the vision expressed in the wish to flourish. To flourish is to venture towards an exemplary life or ideal which society should take after. The celebration of mediocrity in the society is brought out more vividly and glaringly when the poet says' "little mud glitter / and great brains sink into oblivion" (31).

The poet's declaration of his dependence on Kezeh seems to yield nothing. Thus, in "Where Art Thou" the poet engages in a lamentation and rhetorical imploration of the deity Kezeh. Fully conscious that power belongs to Kezeh and not to the "Black vampires", the poet sought for strength from this divine figure to overcome walls of difficulty that threatens to destroy his messianic mission as an artist. In three instances in three stanzas he asks:

> Where art thou my Kezeh,
> Where art thou my fountain
> My patient potent judge?
>
> Where art thou my creator
> Where art thou my father
> My omniscient flawless master?

> Where art thou my Kezeh
> Where art thou my maker
> My fountain and hope? (19-20)

The continuous repetition of the above pattern in the poem, points not necessarily to the longing to know where the deity is but to the wish to feel his presence. Kezeh represents different things to the poet at different instances. At the moment when "foes and woes" connive to disgrace him publicly, Kezeh serves as the image of a "fountain" and "judge". During such moments Kezeh is a fountain of courage to the poet who is about to "stand in public persecution". At the time when others "scheme the demise of the painter", Kezeh is the father and creator. The artist is a creator and so depends on the supreme creator for support. Kezeh here can be considered within the praxis of Bloomian psychoanalyses to be the poet father figure or the belated poet while Ngongkum Ngong is the younger poet. In this line of thought, the poet in question becomes a creator by trying to rewrite or recreate in the example of the elderly poet. It is the supreme creator - Kezeh - that provides the paint and brush which the poet-persona wants to use in repainting the "ribs of his workshop". The image here symbolizes both the poet's mind from where his artistic vision is crafted and the society within which he operates and gains inspiration for writing. In the third instance "moment bitter, moment morbid",

Kezeh is the maker, the foundation and hope. Trapped between gruesome walls and abysmal space, the poet needs a solid foundation of hope to be able to survive especially as the conditions of existence are drowning his courage -"aspirate the courage in my lungs".

There's the sense of fear and reverence in the speaker epitomized in the return to archaic usage "thou" and feeling of ethical force. There is also the personalisation of experience reflected in the use of the possessive genitive of the "I" pronoun "my". Within the modern scope the use of archaic words is more often associated or found in biblical passages or prayers. It is from this perspective that the mystery and reverence of Kezeh can be comprehended. On the other hand, the recurrent use of "My Kezeh" gives the impression that the poet is close to and familiar with the deity. It also shows a degree of emotional attachment between the two. Since Kezeh is an embodiment of everything that the speaker longs for, he shows deep attachment and profound longing for Kezeh by desiring to possess. In "Help Me Help Them" the pattern of rhetorical questions found in "Where Art Thou" gives way to a more direct address in which the poetic inner self is spontaneously asserted in a demand to be taught what is needed to heal the nation. The speaker in this poem speaks from the core of the self. Images derived from his mundane society are turned and placed in the deific consciousness in an attempt to engage the deity in his mission. In "Where Art Thou" the poet is questioning the presence of this spiritual being. He has found Kezeh and so puts the problem to him directly. The poem is thus set in the shrine of Kezeh and opens with the poet reminding the deity of certain salient issues. This is seen below:

> You know the opposition
> And the battle before me,
> The emotions and terrors,
> Digging deep into my bones,
> Threatening to aggravate
> The fissures on my weak walls. (21)

The pressure of evil in the nation is what has pushed the poet to visit and address Kezeh. According to the speaker, Kezeh is not ignorant of the problems. However, the reason for which Kezeh has to remain dormant to the plight of the people until the poet has to remind him is not given. Notwithstanding, as an artist, the poet takes his role as mouthpiece of the people and double as the chief priest of the deity in order to present the plight of the masses. As the title indicates the poet needs help so that he can help his people and nation. The help which the persona needs to fight his people is defined clearly in the poem "Deliver Our Motherland" in which the philosophical poet, Ntongwukuyeh, says his mission is that of exorcising the nation "to deliver this country, our mother/from the talon grip of mercenaries" (Chants, 61) and "to rinse our country in water germfree from the mountain"

(Chants, 68). To be able to achieve such formidable tasks, the poet-persona needs extra help from the supreme realm because he is fighting against what the poet describes in the poem "Wonderful Artist" as "Hawks [that] rummage through the country/looking for newly hatched chicks" (Chants, 77). Conscious of the fact that human force alone cannot undo such evil, the poet-persona confronts Kezeh, the source of the power he needs to accomplish his mission.

The mission which Ntongwukuyeh assigns himself enables him to perform his duty as a poet appropriately. According to Emmanuel Obiechina one of the responsibilities of the poet is to give new life, to revitalize and revive the quality of existence. In "The Writer and his Commitment in Contemporary Nigerian Society", he states that the poet:

> plays the role of conservator as well as destroyer. In the role of conservator of the good values of human society and the destroyer of the values which have ceased to serve the interest of the people, the artist fulfils the function of continually giving new life to the society and invigorating the quality of human existence. (2)

In functioning as the conservator of good values, Ngongkum Ngong thinks that man has to depend on his ancestors or on God. In such a situation, the poet becomes the prophet or mouthpiece of the deities, conveying through imaginative vision the plight of the people to a force that is higher and greater. He therefore engages the divine realm in the struggle to make life meaningful for his people. He pleads with the divine being, Kezeh, to bandage the wounds of his people and give him the strength to be able to restore a worthwhile existence in his nation. The search for divine intervention therefore is aimed at improving "the quality of human existence".

Besides combating the forces of evil and cleansing the nation in germ free water, the poet persona then defines his mission to Kezeh in terms of care for his fellow citizens who have given been battered by the political regime and who have given up the will to live. Though the diction is characterised by imagistic expressions, they all convey the agony of the people and the need for someone to help them. The persona tells the deity exactly what he needs to learn in order to help his people:

> So I have great Kezeh
> To understand how to disinfect
> And bandage stinking laceration (21)

The mission defined in these lines can be interpreted from two perspectives. Firstly, the wish may be to purge the society of the evil that dominates it. The nation is sick or infected and it is the duty of the poet to disinfect and heal it. Secondly he may be to heal the people of the pain that they are going through. Poetry to John Ngongkum Ngong has medicinal value as he says in the poem "Medicinal Brandy" where

Ntongwukuyeh makes the following declarations: "Songs are medicinal.../ Lyrics are curative agents.../ medicinal brandy revives the soul.../ I invite you all quaking with terror/ to destroy fear with medicinal brandy" (*Chants*, 29-30). He wants to become the doctor. The idea of sterilizing and bandaging smelling wounds reveals the humanist instinct of the poet. In situating his second mission he says:

> I have come, immutable father,
> To master how to resuscitate
> And nourish the despondent with hope. (21)

After healing the people/nation, it becomes necessary to give them a light to hold on to-hope. Here the poet shifts from medical imagery to religious imagery. To resuscitate is to resurrect and this often goes with hope in religious thinking. Therefore, he removes the medical jacket and put on the frock or garment of the prophet who like Ezekiel resurrects the dry bones from the valley of death or like Christ calls Lazarus out of the tomb of pain and silence. He cleans their wounds, bandages them and then calls them out of the valley of bereavement and despair. His desire is not just to heal them and then abandon the people. He has to complete his mission by "injecting hope into hopeless souls" (Chants, 61).The hopelessness of the people is a burden in the poet's mind and he needs urgent help from the supreme jurist to be able to extend help to his people. In the final declaration, he says:

> I have come omnipotent jurist

> My mind overwrought, my heart beating
> Weighing my people's crushing wretchedness.
> Help me help them, invincible warrior. (21)

The speaker presents the burden of his people, which weights in his heart. The poem takes its title from the last line and here the help is not from the "great king" or the "immutable father", it is from an "invincible warrior". The invincibility of Kezeh proves the sacredness of the realm from which the poet demands skills and ability to confront the problem of humanity.

The search for divine intervention in the problems of nation does not end with the plea to Kezeh. The poet also implores another deity – Zekembi – to come to his aid. Ngongkum Ngong can thus be said to be prostituting in the realm of duties as he does not stop only at Kezeh and Zekembi but goes as far as engaging Yemenong in the struggle. In "Before Zekembi", we realize that the poet has not been fully fortified for his mission. While he depends on Kezeh for wisdom on how to disinfect a nation infected by moral bankruptcy, corruption, embezzlement and other forms of evil, he depends on Zekembi for courage to face the world and to teach his people. In "Before Zekembi", the title already tells us that the speaker is in front of this deity; it also suggests the idea of waiting which is central in the poem. The persona addresses the deity from a position of respect and reverence:

> Before you Zekembi
> Sustainer of the world,

> Prostate I lie trembling,
> Dying my walls to plaster.
> Before you I prostrate,
> Quaking with fear and tension
> Like rain-beaten chicken
> Yet determined my country serve
> Even in the belly of anguish. (22)

The speaker is lying prostrate before Zekembi. Prostration is a posture of veneration, adoration, and abject submission. It is also a position of exhaustion and complete weakness. Both interpretations and inferences are relevant to the revelation of the poem's meaning. While prostration in front of Zekembi is a mark of reverence for the deity, it is also one of exhaustion from the problems of the nation. Even though he is exhausted and filled with fear and tension, he is still determined to save his nation. He offers himself as a sacrifice for the sake of the people. "I die to tell the world /How lethal fear can be...I die to make my people see / The danger of stitching our mouths" (22). The poet goes through hardship and difficulties just to teach his people the deadlines of fear, and the danger of being silent in the face of immorality. This is why in "Medicinal Brandy" he invites the people "to destroy fear with medicinal brandy" (Chants, 30). He carries the wounds of hardship to the shrine of Zekembi for comfort and for fortification with the "hammer and the word" which he needs to fight tyranny. His wish is that by the time he gets out of arena of Zekembi, he should be strong enough to plant courage in the mind of his countrymen and women and use the poetic art to disperse fear out of their minds.

The quest for strength from deities is also the subject matter of "Yemenong". The poet visits the great river after the rains to see how it ejects dirt particles. At other times, the poet burdened with shame and bitterness moves to the banks to ponder the solemnity of the river in the dry season. The supplication for strength is announced in the third and last stanza:

> Lend me, Yemenong
> The strength in your veins.
> Lend me, O great river
> Your strength whose tough muscles
> In the heart of the rainy season
> Beat hollow, timber fell in to you.
> Lend me your strength wondrous Yemenong
> That I may my crumbling walls rebuild. (44)

For the poet to rebuild a nation in which moral values have crumbled, he needs strength that is comparable to that of the river. The repetition of "lend me" three times within eight lines shows the urgency with which he needs the strength.

An issue that demands examination as far as the quest for divine intervention is concerned is the poet's relationship with the deities. Who are these deities? Are they household gods, one's *Chi* as Achebe will call them? Are they biblical parallels culturalised? Or are they artistic creations for aesthetic self-gratification? Based on the Trinitarian conception and the functions of the deities, they appear to be culturalised parallels of the Christian trinity. In the collection of poems, three deities are invoked at different instances. These are reminiscences of the biblical Trinity of Father, Son and Holy Spirit with Kezeh being the Father, Zekembi being the Son and Yemenong being the Holy Ghost. Kezeh is described variously as "father", "Creator" and "maker" in "Where Art Thou?" as the source of power in "Powerless", and as the giver and taker of life in "Plea". His supremacy over the other deities is equally evident in his frequent recurrence.

Zekembi is a parallel of God the Son as he is reflected in terms that do not place him in equal majesty with Kezeh. In the poem "Before Zekembi", Zekembi is described as "comfort of the wounded", and in "Bandage Our Wounds" he is the "great physician". This description aligns Zekembi to God the Son in that both share the value of healing. While Jesus heals the wounds of blindness, lameness and speechlessness for the people of Israel, Zekembi bandages wounds of torture, affliction and anguish in Cameroon. The perception of Yemenong as a great river with force and strength but that runs with stillness is equal to the perception of the Holy Ghost as fire that burns without faggots. Just as a Christian evokes the Holy Spirit for strength in spiritual battles, so does the poet induces Yemenong for strength in the poetic battle and struggle to rebuild a morally crumbling nation.

Christian religious epistemology and psychology, and aesthetics propose an intrinsic, organic trinity of corresponding majesty and divinity between the Father, Son and Holy Spirit. In this collection, Ngongkum Ngong in his mission of exorcizing the nation, comforting his people and providing a vision of hope builds a similar Trinitarian divine pattern to assist him through. The culturalisation of the Christian God pattern is an artistic strength that is worth saluting. By renaming the godhead and assigning them duties that are relevant to his society, the poet succeeds in communicating his hybrid identity and consciousness about the realms of spirituality - the African and the Western. One issue stands out, whether they are household gods or culturalised biblical parallels, they are at some length artistic creations for self-gratification. The very fact that they have been employed in art makes them to serve an aesthetic function and gives the poet the power of a higher and more sublime realm. The poems leave us with a solemn sense of the importance and essential value which we attribute to forces larger than us be they traditional or Christian.

The poet's dependence and interaction with divine beings brings him to a moment of intuitive insight. The insight constitutes acts of genuine signification and proceeds from human knowledge to the highest human faculty of cognition and recognition, which philosophers refer to as transcendental Reason and artists call the Imagination. The mythic religious response to the moral and social crisis in the poet's nation is an attempt to ground sureness and heal humanity not through reason or institutional systems of belief but in the felt experience of the individual poet as he interrelates with the deities. The search for a solution, through divine intervention, is not in the powers of induction and deduction but in the personal intuition or sublime realms of the universal in the particulars of experience.

Profoundly eloquent with a touch of human feeling and appealing to the sense of truth and justice, the poet's message carry with it an undertone of something sublime within and beyond the words that leaves the reader pondering on the possibilities of depending on deities and responsibility of the deities in providing solutions to the problems that plague the postcolonial nation. To read the poems in which the poet engages in this divine search, and to ponder over the simple but sophisticated diction, the direct and assuaging tone is likely to end in the absorption of the reader in which case the reader identifies himself with the speaker in these poems to the extent that he may see himself in the very truth as the archetypal African man addressing the pain, frustration and anguish of life to an ancestral being.

CONCLUSION

Postcolonial disenchantment has provided discursive space from which both writers and critics take positions of focalization and diagnose the grisly and bitter realities of the postcolonial nation. The horror and terror of post-independence years has worked upon the sensibilities and sensitivities of the writers and has produced varied results. Ayo A. Coly rightly postulates that "Scholars of the nationalism have demonstrated that domestic and familial metaphors are instrumental to the nationalist objectives of naturalizing the nation and constructing loyal and patriotic subjects of the nation (*The Pull*, 41). Postcolonial writers therefore manipulate the "familiar metaphors" to lament the loss of the utopia which was supposed to characterize the postcolonial nation.

This study has explored the works of seven poets - examining their measures, their attitudes, their reliance on history/myth/lore and their methods of word arrangement - in search of the profound subject of nation and nationhood, not just for arguments, but for new materials and ways of expressing the argument. There is an air of plausibility in the philosophical reasoning and notions propagated by each of the poets. Derived from the traumatic and horrific sphere of realistic ordinary experience, these poets extrapolate their ideas into the global terrain of creative and critical discourses on nationhood in ways that are titillating and thought-provoking. Through great variety of considerations and a painful, complicated, yet comprehensive survey of a very complicated matter relating to their identity, belonging and position in the Cameroon nation, these poets come across strongly as representative voices of the literature (poetry) of an unknown nation.

The analysis in this study is representative of the complete spectrum and experience in Anglophone Cameroon poetry because it examines this complex subject in the works of poets from different generations – three Post-Folonians and four New Deal poets. Nol Alembong is representative of the first group of Post-Folonian poets. Other poets in this generation include Tanla Kishani, Germanus Nchanji and Bole Butake. The major defining characteristic of these poets is that they are Oralist poets because much of their poetry is informed by oral traditional imagination. Little wonder therefore and rightly so that Alembong's vision of the nation is couched in forest imagery and folkloric metaphors. The second group of Post-Folonian poets is represented by Alobwed'Epie and the EduArt award-wining poet John Ngongkum Ngong. Other poets in this generation include: Bate

Besong, John Nkemngong Nkengasong, Babila Mutia and Matthew Takwi. The defining characteristic of this group is that their poetry is highly committed and confrontational in the way it treats themes especially those related to the place and position of the Anglophone in Cameroon. Evidently, Alobwed'Epie calls for an open revolution, while John Ngongkum Ngong diagnoses the ills and seeks to purge the nation of evil emblematized by leadership. The New Deal is represented by Dzekashu MacViban, Nyaa Hans Ndah, Sampson Nkwetatang and Gwedeng Ngalah. Other poets in this generation include: the EduArt award-winning poet Wirndzerem G. Barfee, Louisa Lum, and Nsah Mala. These are the poets whom according to Oscar C. Labang constitute

> a generation whose vision of life has been wrought under the grip of a tyrannical and fear instilling antidemocratic regime in the vestments of "advanced democrats". Most of the poets were born in the last hours of the Ahidjo regime and the early days of the Biya's (New Deal). They look back in anger upon the events of more than Twenty Five Years of horror and hopelessness, and diagnose the grossly tribalised, anti-human and vulgar situation in their society. They have witnessed suffering and are still suffering in the hands of highly propagandist politicians and are therefore hostile towards the regime and sceptical about whatever it offers as solutions. (*Emerging Voices*, 12-13)

Wirndzerem G. Barfee situates his generation within a technological matrix. He says they are people that write with "the consciousness of a writer growing and writing in a globalizing age, trying to enracinate local experiences and memory while at the same time negotiating the ineluctability of global influences and values (Barfee). This generation takes the cue from late (second group) Post-Folonians and continue to indict a system of leadership that divides and marginalizes some of the people in the nation. While Dzekashu is concerned with the failure of the bond of brotherhood between the two Cameroon's, Nyaa Hans Ndah takes a more global perspective by condemning leadership failure in Africa with occasional recurs to the Cameroon experience. While like most Cameroonian youth today Ngalah seeks solace in the uniting force of football, Nkwetatang spits prophetic hot-coal on those that have turned the nation into derelict. These poets, put together, represent what George Nyamndi in "Absented Presences in Recent Anglophone-Cameroon Poetry" describes as "the underlying temper of Anglophone consciousness" (3).

In the eight chapters that make up the study, the analysis of issues of nation, and nationalism continually shift from chapter to chapter depending on the major inclination in the work under examination. Chapter one establishes the background, showing how Anglophone Cameroon poetry is not just postcolonial poetry but the poetry of a people undergoing new forms of subjugation in the nation to which they belong. It also briefly explores the nation of nationhood and nationalism as perceived by the Anglophones in Cameroon and as expressed in their poetry. In the second chapter the analysis has established that Nol Alembong successfully conveys a vision of Cameroon and its national history via the manipulation of the image of the forest. Depending heavily on proverbs, traditional images and local metaphors he establishes close association between the making of the forest and the making of Cameroon. The technique of association enables Alembong reveal the different periods or stages that the Cameroon nation has undergone in the journey of nationhood. The poet traces, with fascinating poetic details, the historical experiences of his people and represents the difficulties of living in Cameroon especially as an Anglophone. The third chapter analysis the poetry of Sampson Nkwetatang in the context of apocalyptic literature with the aim of showing that poetry to Nkwetatang is an instrument with multiple functions but the most recurrent function is to curse those who have ruined the postcolonial Cameroon nation and to offer a supplication for God to intervene. The chapter is based on the premise that in "Malediction Upon the Wicked *(Who Have Ruined Cameroon)*", Nkwetatang comes out forcefully and convincingly as an apocalyptic voice announcing doom and seeking salvation or rebirth for the postcolonial Cameroon nation. In the fourth chapter, the analysis focuses on the crisis of leadership as a central concern in Nyaa Hans Ndah's poetry as expressed in his maiden collection *My Africa*. It shows that Ndah's central concern is criticizing the power structure through imaginative creative patterns that reveal the evils of the ruling elite and how they cripple the nation.

Alobwed'Epie's poetry is the subject of chapter five. It argues that the poet builds from the innate part of his being, the opinion that only radical revolutionary action from the masses can restore the beauty of the postcolonial Cameroon nation. Such a revolution, Alobwed'Epie believes, will provide avenues for the construction of new vision for the nation. Alobwed'Epie's intension is to fight the devils that have taken hold of his people in the postcolonial Cameroon nation. The sixth chapter continues the discourse, as expressed in the poetry of Dzekashu MacViban, on how Anglophone Cameroon poetry and poets vocalize the dynamics of the problematic relationship. The analysis shows that the same concerns that are dominant in the poetry of earlier generations of Anglophone Cameroon poets equally find echoes in the poetry of the young Third Generation poet. It shows that issues of identity, belonging and betrayal are topical issues and that the young poet is committed to the course of his people in a manner similar to that of his poetic forebears.

In chapter seven the analysis shifts from the thematic focus to a stylistic one as in chapter two. But in this chapter the focus is on symbolism. To achieve this, the chapter examines Gwedeng Ngalah as one of the most prolific aestheticians in Anglophone Cameroon poetry. The poetry of Ngalah has the potential to attract false impression that he is more concerned with aesthetic twists than with the crucial issues rocking the nation. But underneath the aesthetic twist lies his prowess as a poet – the ability to weave themes that are central to his people and to humankind with fine imaginative and inventive playfulness. The chapter is based on the premise that in some of his poems Ngalah manipulates a series of symbols to convey a message of hope and unity for the Cameroon nation. To read an Anglophone Cameroon poetry that postulates hope and calls for a united Cameroon at a time when the general tendency is to castigate the status-quo is somewhat intriguing. The final chapter examines the poetry of John Ngongkum Ngong in the light of the poet's attempt to invoke divine forces to help him purge the nation of the evil that has ruined it. In his poetry, Ngongkum Ngong summons mythic reality through a horizon of spirituality in an attempt to harmonize the world of banal inanities that typifies the postcolonial Cameroon nation.

This study sought to expand the field of postcolonial literary discussion on nation and nationalism by exploring how postcolonial Anglophone poetry, much like postcolonial fiction, represents the text and context of postcolonial nationhood. The postulations of critics like Fredric Jameson that fiction represents the nation, has given rise to several studies of the postcolonial nation in fiction under the assumption that poetry is allusive, compressed and obscure especially in terms of reference to the society. This study has shown that contrary to this, postcolonial poetry, though compressed, and allusive with ironical, paradoxical and multidimensional images and proverbs, is capable of engaging social concerns as well as reflecting or interrogating the postcolonial nation. The choice to study each poet in a separate chapter is intended to give each of the poets a distinctive significance. Each chapter pays close attention and gives analytical seriousness to a particular aspect of nationhood and nationalism, thereby projecting the poets as prototypical figures of the passions and anxieties that animate postcolonial Anglophone Cameroon poetry. Thus, these poets signify contemporary reality and express the consciousness of the Anglophone with a passion that is common only to people who know the bitter truth of being a second-class citizen in their nation.

NOTES

[i] *Beast of No Nation* is the title of the play by Bate Besong which earned him a moment of imprisonment and the banning of theatrical performance in Cameroon for a long time. The play is notoriously radical in its presentation of the disenfranchised and second-class status of Anglophone Cameroonians. It is used here to show the backward progression of Anglophone identity since independence, which was achieved by joining the already independent French Cameroon.

[ii] Elleke Boehmer in his 1998 essay "Endings and New Beginning: South African Fiction in Transition" in *Writing South Africa: Literature, Apartheid and Democracy* edited by Derek Attridge and Rosemary Jolly, and published by Cambridge University Press.

[iii] Benedict Anderson's monumental book *Imagined Communities: Reflections on the Origin and Spread of Nationalism* published in London by Verso is one of the sources that provide an authoritative discourse on the idea of nation and nationalism.

[iv] In *WB Yeats, Realms of Romantic Imagination*, John Nkemngong Nkengasong explores the concept of Romantic imagination briefly from the perspective of Samuel Coleridge as defined in *Biographia Literaria*, then extends to other views like divinity of the imagination as considered by Blake. Even more interesting is his idea of the imagination as represented in Yeats' poetry where "the imagination becomes a means of emancipating oneself from any form of life that is traumatizing and frustrating" (7).

[v] Ernest Renan's essay "What is a Nation?" in *Nation and Narration* edited by Homi K. Bhabha and published in London by Routledge, sees the nation as a soul or spiritual principal that is made up of a past and a present.

[vi] The excerpt from Desmond Tutu's book *No Future Without Forgiveness* is a reference to the necessity for forgiveness in the post-apartheid South African nation. It is used here to show that for a nation in which one segment has once subjugated another to inhuman and mean treatment to survive, there must be the affirmation of the "dignity and personhood" of the marginalized persons.

[vii] McCallum Shara discusses the notion of exile from the perspective of Derek Walcott's assertion about V. S. Naipaul that "either every writer is an exile ... or no writer is". To Shara exile is a common phenomenon in Caribbean writing and Walcott does not see it in terms of moving beyond one's national boundaries. It is rather a self-conscious state that makes the writer feel alienated or dislocated.

[viii] References from Emmanuel Anyambod are from his unpublished paper presented during the book launch.

[ix] Wirndzerem G. Barfee is author of a poetry collection titled *Voice of the Oracular Verb* published by Iroko Publishers, Yaounde, 2008. He is a winner of the EduArt Award.

[x] Ernest Veyu is author of four poetry collections published by Miraclaire Publishing and Darenehope publication. He writes dominantly religious poetry with a touch similar to that of the English poet John Donne.

BIBLIOGRAPHY

Alembong, Nol. *Forest Echoes*. Kansas City and Yaoundé: Miraclaire Publishing, 2012. Print.
All Anglophone Conferences Standing Committee. *The Buea Declaration*. Limbe: Nooremac Press, 1993. Print.
Alobwed'Epie. *Crying in Hiccoughs*. Bamenda: Langaa, 2011. Print.
Ambanasom, Shadrach. "Bate Besong: Is His Poetry Too Difficult For Cameroonians?" *African Literature Association (ALA) Bulletin*. 28. 3/4. Summer/Fall 2000.1-10. Print.
Ambe, Hilarious. "The Anglophone-Francophone Marriage and Anglophone Dramatic Compositions in the Cameroon Republic". *Towards a Transcultural Future: Literature and Human Rights in a 'Post'-Colonial World*. Eds. Peter M. Marsden & Geoffrey V. Davis. New York: Rodopi, 2004.71-80. Print.
Anderson, Benedict. *Imagined Communities: Reflections on the Origin and Spread of Nationalism*. London: Verso, 1983. Print.
Ashcroft, Bill. "Beyond the Nation: Post-Colonial Hope". *The Journal of the European*

Association of Studies on Australia.1. 2009. 12-22. Print.

Auden, Wystan Hugh. *Collected Poems*. Ed. Edward Mendelson. New York: Vintage Books, 1991. Print.

Barfee, Wirndzerem Gideon. *Bird of the Oracular Verb*. Yaounde: Iroko Publishing, 2008. Print.

__ __ __. "Dearth and Death: The Growing Lacuna in Cameroon Anglophone Literary Criticism and Debate". *Palapala Magazine*. 4. 2009. Web. February 2010.

Bennis, W.G. "The Seven Stages of Leadership". *Harvard Business Review*. 82.1. 2004. 46-53. Print.

Berger, James. "Twentieth-century Apocalypse: Forecasts and Aftermaths". *Twentieth Century Literature*. 46. 4. 2000. 387-395. Print.

Besong, Bate. *The Grain of Bobe Ngom Jua.* Yaounde: Drapoe, 1986. Print.

__ __ __. *Beast of No Nation*. Limbe: Nooremac, 1991. Print.

__ __ __. "Post –Unification Anglophone Exile Poetry: Introducing Simon Mol & Kangsen Feka Wakai". *Bate Besong: Freedom Ink.* June 19, 2006. Web. June 2012.

Bobda, Augustine Simo. "Varying Perception of English in Cameroon: A Diachronic and Synchronic analysis". *TRANS. Internet-*

Zeitschriftfür Kulturwissenschaften. 11.2001. Web. April 2012.

Boehmer, Elleke. "Endings and New Beginning: South African Fiction in Transition". *Writing South Africa: Literature, Apartheid and Democracy.* ed. Derek Attridge and Rosemary Jolly. Cambridge: Cambridge University Press, 1998. 43-56. Print.

Book of Isaiah. The King James 2000 Bible. Robert A. Couric. *Online Bible.* Web. August15, 2012.

Book of Jeremiah. The King James 2000 Bible. Robert A. Couric. *Online Bible.* Web. August15, 2012.

Book of Revelation. The King James 2000 Bible. Robert A. Couric. *Online Bible.* Web. August15, 2012.

Brennan, Timothy. "The National Longing for Form". *Nation and Narration.* Ed. Homi Bhabha. London: Routledge, 1990. Print.

Butake, Bole. *Family Saga.* Yaoundé: Edition Cle, 2005. Print.

_____. *Betrothal Without Libation.* Yaoundé: Edition Cle, 2005. Print.

Carter, John W. "God's Plan for Persecuted Believers". *American Journal of Biblical Theology.* 1. March 6, 2000. 52. Print.

_____. "An Introduction to the Interpretation of Apocalyptic Literature". *American Journal of*

Biblical Theology, 1 (2007). August 15, 2011. Web.

Collins, Adela Y. "The Early Christian Apocalypses". *Semeia*. 14. 1979. Print.

Collier, Paul and Anke E. Hoeffler. "On the Incidence of Civil War in Africa." November 2009. Web.

Coly, Ayo. *The Pull of the postcolonial Nation: Gender and Migration in Francophone African Literature.* Maryland: Lexington Books, 2010. Print.

Cott, Nancy F. *The Grounding of Modern Feminism.* New Haven: Yale University Press, 1987. Print.

"Deuteronomy". *Good News Translation*. 2nd Ed. American Bible Society, 1992. Print.

Doh, Emmanuel Fru. "Foreword". *Forest Echoes*. Nol Alembong. Kansas City and Yaounde: Miraclaire Publishing, 2012. i-vii. Print.

Eliot, T.S. *Selected Essays.* London: Faber, 1932. Print.

Heffernan, Teresa. "Apocalyptic Narratives: The Nation in Salman Rushdie's *Midnight's Children"*. *Twentieth-Century Literature* 46. 4. 2000. 470-491. *Contemporary Literary Criticism*. Ed. Tom Burns and Jeffrey W. Hunter. Vol. 191. Detroit: Gale, 2004. *Literature Resource Center*. 11 Aug. 2012.

Fokem, Sam Nuvala. "Cameroon/Egypt: Snapshot - Pharaoh, Let My People Go!" February 17, 2008. Web. October 9, 2009.

Friend, Celeste. "The Social Contract". *Internet Encyclopedia of Philosophy*: *A Peer-Review Academic Resource.* October 15, 2004. Web. February 28, 2012.

Gandhi, Leela. *Postcolonial Theory: A Critical Introduction.* Sydney: Allen & Unwin, 1998.

"Genesis". *Good News Translation.* 2nd Ed. American Bible Society, 1992. Print.

Gill, Rosalind. "Postfeminist Media Culture: Elements of A Sensibility". *European journal of cultural studies.* 10 2. 2007. 147-166. Print.

Graves, Robert. *The Complete Poems.* ed. Beryl Graves and Dunstan Ward. London: Penguin, 2003. Print.

Gwedeng, Ngalah. *Cameroon My All.* Yaounde: Miraclaire Publishing, 2009.

Hardy, Thomas. "Nature Questioning". *Thomas Hardy: Selected Poems.* Ed. Walford Davies. London: Everyman's, 1982.

Harris, Robert A. "Anaphora". *A Handbook of Rhetorical Devices.* January 5, 2010. Web. December 2011.

Hawkins, Virgil. *"What's Death got to do with it?" Stealth Conflicts. December 12, 2008.* web. November 10. 2011.

Hungwe, Elda and Chipo Hungwe. "Interrogating Notions of Nationhood, Nation and Globalisation in Postcolonial Africa: A Textual Analysis of Four African Novels". *452°F. Electronic journal of theory of literature and comparative literature*. 2. 2010. 30-47. Print.

Invictus. Dir. Clint Eastwood, 2009.

Jua, Nantang and Piet Konings. "Occupation of Public Space Anglophone Nationalism in Cameroon". *Cahiers d'Études Africaines*. 44. 175. 2004. 609-633. Print.

Katz, Jack *How Emotions Work*. Chicago: University of Chicago Press, 1999.

Konings, Piet and Francis Nyamjoh. "Construction and Deconstruction: Anglophones or Autochtones". *The African Anthropologist*. 7.1. 2000. Print.

Kor, Buma. "The Literature of the Hunchback." *Anglophone Cameroon Writing: WEKA*. Breitinger, Butake, and Lyonga. Bayreuth; Bayreuth University Press, 1993. 60-75. Print.

Kövecses, Zoltán. *Metaphor: A Practical Introduction*. Oxford: Oxford University Press, 2002. Print.

Labang, Oscar. "Waiting For a Declaration". *My Country Took A Wrong Turn*. Yaounde: Miraclaire Publishing, 2011. Print.

___ __ __. "Introduction". *Songs for Tomorrow: Cameroon Poetry in English*. Yaounde: Miraclaire Publishing, 2010. i – iv.

———. "Foreword". *The Sex Allegory (And Other Poems)*. Yaounde: Miraclaire Publishing, 2011. vi-vii. Print.

———. "Introduction". *Emerging Voices: Anthology of Young Anglophone Cameroon Poets.* Yaounde: Miraclaire Publishing, 2008. Print.

Langer, G. "Water's Edge: Greater Trust in Government Limited to National Security". *ABCNews.com*. January 14, 2004. Web. March 2012.

Lakoff, George, and Mark Johnson. *Metaphors We Live By.* Chicago: University of Chicago, 1980. Print.

Loomba, Ania. Colonialism and Post-Colonialism. London: Rutledge, 1998.

Lum, Louisa. "These Feminist Clowns". *The Sex Allegory (And Other Poems)*. Yaoundé: Miraclaire Publishing, 2011. 40-41. Print.

Lutz, Tom *Crying: The Natural and Cultural History of Tears*. 1. Ed. New York: Norton, 1999. Print.

MacViban, Dzekashu. *Scions of the Malcontent.* Yaoundé: Miraclaire Publishing, 2011. Print.

———. "These Feminists Clowns: A Review of Louisa Lum's *The Sex Allegory*". *FabAfriq*. December 2011. Web. January 15, 2012.

Marx, Karl. "On the Jewish Question." *The Marx-Engels Reader*. Ed. Robert C. Tucker. New York: Norton, 1978. 26-52. Print.

McCallum, Shara. "'Either I'm Nobody or I'm a Nation': Derek Walcott's Poetry." *The Antioch Review* Winter 2009: 22+. *Literature Resource Center.* Web. August 11, 2012.

McEnery, Tony. *Corpus-based and Computational Approaches to Discourse Anaphora.* Amsterdam: John Benjamins Publishing, 2000. Print.

McRobbie, Angela. *The Aftermath of Feminism: Gender, Culture and Social Change.* Sage Publications, 2009. Print.

___. "Post-Feminism and Popular Culture". *Feminist Media Studies.* 4. 3. 2004. Print.

Merriam-Webster Online Dictionary. 2009. Merriam-Webster Online. Web. October 28, 2009.

Milton, John. *Paradise Lost.* Iowa: 1st World Library, 2003. Print.

Mitchell, T.R. and W.J. Scott. "Leadership Failures, the Distrusting Public and Prospects of the Administrative State". *Public Administration Review.* 47. 6. 1987. 445-452. Print.

Ndah, Nyaa Hans. *My Africa.* Yaounde: Nyaa Publishers, 2008. Print.

Ndobegang, Michael. "The Anglophone-Francophone Divide in Cameroon: Diagnosis of A National Disconnection". July 2009. Web. April 2012.

Ngoh, Victor Julius. ed. *Cameroon: From a Federal to a Unitary State, 1961-1972. A Critical Study.* Limbe: Design House, 2004. Print.

Ngome, Victor Epie. "*What God Has Put Asunder.* Yaoundé: Pitcher Books Ltd., 1992. Print.

Ngong, John Ngongkum in *Walls of Agony*. Yaoundé: Edition Cle, 2007. Print.

_ _ _. *Chants of a Lunatic*. Yaoundé: Edition Cle, 2007. Print.

Nkengasong, John Nkemngong. "Interrogating the Union: Anglophone Cameroon Poetry in the Postcolonial Matrix". *Journal of Postcolonial Writing*. 47.3. 2011. 1-4. Print.

_ _ _. *WB Yeats: Realms of Romantic Imagination*. Germany: Cuvillier Verlag, 2011. Print.

_ _ _. "Anglophone Cameroon Poetry: The Poetics and Politics of the 'New Deal' Regime". *New Urges in Post-Colonial Literature*. Ed. Sunita Sinha. New Delhi: Atlantic Publishers, 2009. 61-75. Print.

_ _ _."Anglophone Cameroon Poetry since 1990: A Critical Perspective". *Cameroun: Nouveau paysage littéraire (Cameroon: New Literary Landscape)*. Ed. Marcelin Vounda Etoa. Yaounde: Editions CLE, 2009. Print.

_ _ _. *Black Caps and Red Feathers*. Bamenda: Patron Publishing, 2004. Print.

_ _ _. *Across the Mongolo*. Ibadan: Spectrum Books Limited, 2004. Print.

———. "Preface". *Walls of Agony*. Yaoundé: Edition Cle, 2006. Print.

Nkwetatang, Sampson. "Malediction Upon the Wicked (Who Have Ruined Cameroon*)*". *Songs for Tomorrow: Cameroon Poetry in English.* 2009 Ed. Oscar C. Labang et.al. Yaoundé: Miraclaire Publishing, 2010. 27-30. Print.

———. "Lord Save Cameroon from Shackles". *The Ngoh-Kuoh Review: Creativity and Criticism*. 1.2. 2011. 32 – 33. Print.

Northhouse, Peter. *Leadership: Theory and Practice*. 5th ed. California: Sage, 2010. Print.

Nwakanma, Obi. "Metonymic Eruptions: Igbo Novelists, The Narrative of the Nation, and New Developments in the Contemporary Nigerian Novel". *Research in African Literatures.* 39. 2. 2008. Print.

Nyamndi, George. "Absented Presences in Recent Anglophone-Cameroon Poetry". *English Academy Review: Southern African Journal of English Studies*. 26. 1. 2009. Print.

Obiechina, Emmanuel. "The Writer and his Commitment in Contemporary Nigerian Society". *Okike: African Journal of New Writing*. 27/28. 1998. 1-9. Print.

O'Donnell, M. ""Bring it on": The Apocalypse of George W. Bush". *Media International*

Australia Incorporating Culture and Policy. 113. 2004. 1 – 31.

Patel, V. "Crying Behavior and Psychiatric Disorder in Adults: A Review". *Comprehensive Psychiatry*. 34. 3. 1993. 206 – 11. Print.

Pateman, Carole. "The Fraternal and Social Contract". *Civil Society and the State: New European Perspectives.* Ed. John Keane. London: Verso, 1988. 101-27. Print.

Renan, Ernest. "What is a Nation?" *Becoming National: A Reader.* ed. Geoff Eley and Ronald Grigor Suny. New York and Oxford: Oxford University Press, 1996. 41-55. Print.

"The Function of Poetry and the Place of the Poet in Society". *World Outside the Window: Selected Essays of Kenneth Rexroth*. New Directions Publishing Corp., 1987. Web. July 7, 2012.

Richards, I. A. *The Philosophy of Rhetoric*. Oxford: Oxford University Press, 1936. Print.

Rose, Eugene (Fr Seraphine). *Nihilism: The Root of the Revolution of the Modern Age*. Web. June 6, 2012.

Said, Edward. *Culture and Imperialism*. London: Chatto & Windus, 1993. Print.

Sandler, Lauren. "Why do More Women than Men Still Belief in God?" *Double X*. October 12, 2009. Web. October 28, 2012.

Shah, Anup. "Conflicts in Africa – Introduction." *Global Issues: Social, Political, Economic and Environmental Issues That Affect Us All.* May 10. 2010. Web. January 10, 2012.

Shoumatoff, Alex. *African Madness.* New York: Alfred A. Knopf, 1988. Print.

Sommers, Marc. "Urbanization, War, and Africa's Youth at Risk: Towards Understanding and Addressing Future Challenges". *Basic Education and Policy Support (BEPS) Activity.* US Agency for International Development, 2003. Print.

The Stockholm International Peace Research Institute. *Yearbook of World Armaments and Disarmaments.* Oxford: Oxford University Press, 1999.

Suter, Anthony. "Time and the Literary Past in the Poetry of Basil Bunting". *Contemporary Literature.* 12. 4. 1971. 510 – 526. Print.

Tognini-Bonelli, Elena. *Corpus Linguistics at Work.* Amsterdam: John Benjamins Publishing, 2001. Print.

Trotsky, Leon. "The Social Roots and the Social Function of Literature (1923)". *Philosophy / History Archive.* January 6, 2007. Web. May 2012.

Tutu, Desmond. *No Future without Forgiveness.* New York: Doubleday, 2000. Print.

"The Waves of Feminism". *Moving Toyshop.*
    September 7, 2010. Web. December 2011.
Yeats, W.B. "The Second Coming". *The Collected Poems of W.B. Yeats*. London: Macmillan, 1965. Print.

Name Index

Achebe
  Chinua, 67, 180
Ahidjo
  Amadou, 59, 146, 187
Alembong
  Nol, viii, 15, 19, 20, 21, 22, 24, 27, 28, 29, 33, 39, 40, 124, 186, 188, 189, 195, 198
Alobwed'Epie, 15, 94, 95, 96, 97, 98, 99, 102, 104, 106, 111, 116, 119, 186, 189, 190
Ambanasom
  Shadrach, viii, 67, 92, 140, 195
Ambe
  Hilarious, 161, 162, 195
Anderson
  Benedict, 4, 6, 9, 10, 66, 195
Anyambod
  Emmanuel A., 91, 92, 194
Ashcroft
  Bill, 17, 195

Ashuntantang
  Joyce, vii
Barfee
  Wirndzerem G., 98, 124, 187, 194, 196
Bennis
  Warren, 77, 196
Berger
  James, 44, 196
Besong
  Bate, 3, 9, 59, 98, 123, 186, 193, 195, 196
Bobda
  Augustine Sime, 121, 197
Boehmer
  Elleke, 2, 10
Brennan
  Timothy, 4, 197
Butake
  Bole, 11, 12, 35, 39, 123, 128, 186, 197, 200
Carter
  John, 60, 198
Collins
  Adela Yarbro, 42, 43, 198

Coly
  Ayo A., 185, 198
Doh
  Emmanuel Fru, vii, 26, 30, 198
Fonkem
  Sam Nuvala, 153, 154
Franzmann
  Martin, 65
Gandhi
  Leela, 6, 7, 8, 13, 14, 17, 199
Goodwin
  Ken, iii
Heffernan
  Teresia, 43, 46, 61, 65, 198
Jua
  Nantang, 120, 123, 196, 200
Katz
  Jack, 112, 113, 200
Kishani
  Tanla, 186
Konings
  Piet, 120, 132, 134, 200
Kor
  Buma, 3, 200

Labang
  Oscar C., i, iii, viii, 29, 77, 104, 106, 133, 138, 187, 201, 204
Loomba, 201
  Ania, 9, 10
Lum
  Louisa, viii, 187, 201, 202
MacViban
  Dzekashu, 15, 72, 73, 74, 120, 124, 125, 126, 127, 130, 138, 187, 190, 202
Mandela
  Nelson, 103, 154
Marx
  Karl, 56, 202
McCallum
  Shara, 43, 194, 202
Ndah
  Nyaa Hans, 15, 67, 69, 70, 71, 72, 75, 77, 80, 84, 88, 91, 187, 188, 189, 203
Ndobegang
  Michael, 121, 122, 203
Ngalah,
  Gwedeng, 16, 140, 141, 144, 145, 148, 149,

150, 154, 164, 165, 187, 188, 190, 199
Ngoh
Victor Julius, 122, 123, 204, 207
Ngome
Victor Epie, 39, 120, 130, 143, 203
Ngong
John Ngongkum, 7, 15, 16, 45, 123, 124, 167, 171, 175, 176, 178, 182, 186, 187, 191, 203
Nkengasong
John Nkemngong, vi, vii, 3, 5, 110, 120, 123, 124, 167, 186, 193, 203
Nkwetatang
Sampson, 15, 42, 43, 44, 45, 46, 47, 48, 49, 50, 51, 52, 53, 54, 55, 56, 58, 59, 60, 61, 62, 65, 187, 188, 189, 204
Northhouse
Peter, 68, 204
Nwakanma
Obi, 4, 204
Nyamjoh
Francis, 132, 134, 200

Nyamndi
George, 188, 205
Obiechina
Emmanuel, 174, 205
Painter
F.V.N, ii, 139
Pateman
Carole, 56, 205
Renan,
Ernest, 7, 10, 11, 12, 13, 193, 205
Rexroth
Kenneth, 100, 206
Richards
I. A., 19, 20, 206
Said
Edward, 12, 206
Tala
Kashim Ibrahim, iv, viii
Tande
Dibussi, ii, vii
Trotsky
Leon, 94, 207
Tutu
Desmond, 13, 207
Vakunta
Peter, vii
Veyu
Ernest, 98, 194
Wakai
Kangsen Feka, vii, 196

Note About Author

Oscar C. Labang holds a PhD in British Literature and has taken courses in the Master of Fine Arts, and Master of Science in Management. He is CEO AND General Manager at Miraclaire Publishing. He is also co-founder and Chairperson of the Cameroon English Language and Literature Association (CELLA). His research interests include: British Literature, postcolonial Anglophone Literatures, theoretical Criticism and Creative Writing. He is author of *Riot in the Mind: A Critical Study of John N. Nkengasong*. He is in the final stages of two other books *Voices and Visions: Contemporary Anglophone Cameroon Poetry* and *T.S. Eliot and W.H. Auden: Existential Disconnectedness and the Search for Connectives*. He publishes a personal journal at www.la-bang.org, dedicated to writing about Anglophone Cameroon Literature.

www.ingramcontent.com/pod-product-compliance
Lightning Source LLC
Chambersburg PA
CBHW021827300426
44114CB00009BA/353